The Boy

from Peru

CHRIS DALE

ISBN:9781535346603

ABOUT THIS BOOK

The Boy from Peru follows the tale of a ten-year-old who is taken out of an idyllic lifestyle living in his country of birth in Lima, Peru, to attend a public boarding school eight thousand miles away in a country that has a totally different culture. It depicts his experiences and adventures as he rebels against his parent's decision to give him a better education.

This book is partly fiction, as some events have been embellished for the reader, but is based on actual experiences of the author.

Quotes

These quotes do illustrate the contents of this book and give relevance.

"Do not train a child to learn by force or harshness; but direct them to it by what amuses their minds, so that you may be better able to discover with accuracy the peculiar bent of the genius of each."

Plato

"I have never let my schooling interfere with my education."

Mark Twain

DEDICATION

To my Mum and Dad …. I miss you.

Thank you for opening my eyes to the real world.

May you rest in peace.

CHARACTERS

Charles Lawrence Dashwood -*Principle Character*

Chris Wrigley – *Best Friend at School – St Kits*

Tobias Mortimer – *USA - gang of five*

Kando Oboke – *Nigeria – gang of five*

Titus la Croix -*French Guyana – gang of five*

Harriet Patricia Dashwood – *Charles's sister*

Auntie Joan Evans - *Guardian*

Mr. Langhorne – *Head Master Drummond College –Cheltenham*

Mr. Rowland – *Maths teacher*

Mademoiselle Fabien – *French teacher*

Mrs. Yates – *English teacher*

Mrs. Ramsbottom -*School Matron*

Dominic Worrall – *Head Boy*

Joshua Ames – *Dormitory Prefect*

Ginger Baines – *Dormitory Prefect*

Rupert de Long – *Dormitory Prefect*

Mrs. Partington-Smythe – *Stable owner*

Millicent (Millie) Partington-Smythe - *Daughter*

Carlos, Maria, Juanita & Consuelo –*house staff in Lima*

Dr. Gonzales – *Peruvian Doctor*

La Croix family in France

Pierre, Louisa, Chantelle, Marie-Clare & Jean-Paul

Sabine Le Croix – *Titus's older sister*

Jean-Claude- *Titus's older brother*

Monsieur Graveaux – *Farming friend and pilot*

Clive, Carlos & Ben -*Lima school friends*

ACKNOWLEDGMENTS

To my big sister, Trisha for help in jogging my memory; to my Dad for providing valuable information in his book, "A Taste of Adventure," which he wrote in 1993; to John Kain for his guidance in all things Peruvian and for proof reading this as well, and to Jan Cook for checking the spelling!

CHAPTER ONE
THE EARLY DAYS

Peru – a Spanish influenced country on the west coast of South America, with the Pacific Ocean and Humboldt Current running up one side, and bordered by Ecuador, Colombia, Brazil, Bolivia and Chile. It is a wonderful country with every climatic element you could have, mountains, seas, jungle and deserts. The Spanish spoken here is Castilian, and French is the second most prominent language. You can fit the UK ten times into Peru I am told, so it's quite a big country.

I want to paint you a picture of my early life, before we get to the main story, as it's important that you see and feel the background of my upbringing.

I was born here in Lima on 7th January 1954 at 2.20 in the morning; 10lbs 10 oz., to British parents living and working as ex-pats. My childhood life was a dream really – living what could be called a false life in a country that had three social classes, you were either rich, poor or ex-pat.

I have an older sister Harriet, and our mum who was a trained nurse, worked at the local American

Hospital and taught as well at Kindergarten.

My early life was ideal on a typical day, I got up and went to school at seven am, was collected at twelve to go to the beach for lunch, and dropped off at school again at four until six thirty; then home for supper and bed. You should understand the basic differences between the UK and Peru. Summer there was from November to February and the temperature gets into the low 90's F (30 C), and winter was May to August, when it was cooler (well relatively to us, in the 60'sF (16C) and dull, damp and often very foggy.

However, when it was hot on the coast it was cool in the mountains and vice versa.

At weekends, there were several clubs we belonged to as a family, so we spent our time either at the Lima Cricket Club in town or the Country Club de Villa on the coast. I learnt to swim before I could walk, and in the Pacific Ocean, although cold was our learning pool. We also had a swimming pool at home of course and I was taught to swim competitively at the Country Club by a German teacher, who refined our stroke so that we could swim gracefully and at speed in all four; crawl, backstroke, breast and butterfly. I was also taught 'old English' backstroke, which became my favourite.

We were then entered swimming competitions which I was always very good at.

The food was very different to that of the UK. We ate creole or BBQ-style all the time and the food was delicious, with sweet potatoes, rice and noodles being the staple diet, together with corn, maize, peas and asparagus. We ate plenty of beef, chicken, pork and Guinea pigs, fish and seafood. Watermelons, pineapples, oranges and kiwi were the main staple diet of fruit we ate. A typical breakfast was watermelon, croissants and cornflakes with 'leche gloria', an evaporated tin milk, as pasteurised milk went off too quickly in the heat and humidity. Lunch was always a pita bread sandwich of meats or a BBQ; and dinner always had a rice- based meal.

I had loads of good friends at school and we used to have the freedom to go where we liked, bareback riding on the beach, or sand sailing in the deserts, or river rafting in the mountains.

We had the use of a ranch in the Cordillera Blanca, which was run by local farmers as a co-operative that we went to for long weekends or for short holidays.

It was wild country and a horse was your best friend together with hunting dogs that kept you safe from the pumas and mountain lions that roamed freely.

In the winter months, we would spend weekends at the Granja Azul in Chosica up in the mountains, where we went horse-riding again, and ate BBQ chicken roasted on spits with chips. Chicken was all the food they cooked and they had these giant walls of charcoal that held row upon row of whole chickens on spits, probably ten chickens to each spit. These were slowly turned by a series of cogs attached to a giant wheel with a donkey turning it round. The chef and his assistants would baste the chickens frequently until they were cooked, then slide them off the spits and chop them into four with a massive meat cleaver. We each were served at trestle tables with wooden bowls and two quarters of deliciously roasted chicken with potato chips and a cooked corn cob. There were no knives and forks, so you ate with your hands and had bowls of lemon water and giant napkins to clean yourself with. It was simply delicious!!

In the first ten years of my life we had moved home several times in Lima, but the one we spent most of our time at was in Gonzales Larrañaga in the suburb of Miraflores. Our house was a single- story building with a flat roof, which housed a small apartment made up of three bedrooms, a bathroom and a sitting room – this is where the staff lived. The main house had four bedrooms, two bathrooms, one was end suite with our parent's room. We had a dining room, a study, a kitchen and a huge open plan sitting room. The sitting room covered the whole house from front door to back door with the bedrooms on each side of it. We didn't have carpets due to the bugs, so all the floors were parquet wooden floors, all highly polished, with rugs or throws covering certain areas. There were huge gaps between the floor and the top of the skirting board, where, spiders, scorpions, cockroaches, huge centipedes and other insects lived. It was great fun catching them. They made great entertainment when I took them to school to show the teachers. Especially the female ones or the cissy boys.

Harriet also hated all the insects, so I took delight in putting some in her bed at night.

At night during the summer months, we had to sleep under mosquito nets at night to stop them from biting us as we slept, but it was so hot and humid in the summer months that I used to sleep without any clothes on, despite being regularly told off by mother or Juanita.

Carlos and Maria, were a husband and wife team; they were traditional Peruvian Indians from the mountain regions and originally came from Cuzco. They were direct descendants from the Incas and they spoke both Quechua (the original Inca language spoken in the Andes) as well as Spanish. Carlos was Dad's chauffeur; doubled as the gardener and when Mum and Dad held dinners or cocktail parties at home he became our butler. Maria was an excellent cook and kept us well fed, with different food for Harriet and me as from our parents. Juana (Juanita as we called her) their daughter was a housemaid as well as our nanny, and their cousin Consuelo, did general house work. Juana spent the most time with us and took me to school every morning, Harriet was collected by her school bus, and I generally made my own way home.

◆◆

Dad was an English engineer, based in Lima, but working all over South America selling the engines his company produced to every industry going; mining, fishing fleets, hydro-electric power, desalinization pumps, irrigation for cotton and banana plantations, and he sold ex-navy war ships too. A remarkable man from Lincoln. Although Dad travelled a lot and was away from home for weeks at a time *(remember that in the fifties and sixties, air travel was slow on DC3s and DC4s or it was by steam train or ship)*. We had a grand life style, mixing with a wide community of English, French, German, Italian and American families, together with native Peruvians, but the language was always in Spanish. We were fortunate that our parents could take us all over Peru and we visited the ancient Inca temples in Cuzco, Macchu Pichu, Sacsayhuaman, the Nazca lines, and down to Arequipa near Lake Titicaca. Iquitos in the jungle was the scariest, because of all the creatures, insects, and the sheer humidity.

We had a small walled garden at home, where I used to set traps to catch local insects such as scorpions, tarantula spiders and giant ants. I put these in a box and watched fascinated for hours the ensuing battle between them. The dead ones I put in my sister's bed, just as a joke!

In the late fifties in South America there was little danger of kidnaps or violent crimes, so it was relatively safe, but we were accompanied wherever we went by either Juana, Consuelo or driven by Carlos. All my friend's families also had staff and chauffeurs so we were never short on lifts.

I was very happy. I went to a great school, had fantastic friends, and lived a very exciting life going from one house party to a beach party, and occasionally we accompanied Mum and Dad to one business event or another, where families were very much welcomed.

From a social side, the Peruvians were past masters of supporting the phrase 'manana' (meaning tomorrow), as they were always bad timekeepers. So traditionally if you sent an invitation to come to a party at 12 o'clock, they would turn up at two. Dad had a saying 'hora Inglsa y hora Peruana' (meaning English time and Peruvian time); when they had cocktail parties at home or organised events at the clubs, they always sent out two invitations; one to the Europeans and Americans stating the right time, and one to the Peruvians and other South Americans stating a time two hours before the official start time. That way their parties always started with everyone there on time. This was the way of life out there, if you agreed to meet someone at 2pm, it was acceptable to be anything up to three hours late in arriving.

We didn't have any televisions- black and white TV had just arrived in Peru, but Dad wouldn't buy one. We used the gramophone, radio and tape recorder. The cinema was a drive-in open-air type on the outskirts of San Isidro the region of Lima suburbs we lived in. There were four cinemas around the capital Lima, all were open air.

I was always fascinated by aviation and would either cycle or horseback ride with my school buddies to Limatambo Airport in San Isidro, very near to where we lived; the city's main airport which was also used by the Peruvian Air Force. Here we would watch all the activity of both civil and air force aircraft, mostly turbo prop, but they did have ex-RAF and US Air force jets, such as Canberra's, Hunters, Lightening's, and F 1-11 and F3 fighters. Based there were also several flying boats that were used for water bombing to extinguish fires. But in 1960 the airport was closed for housing development because it was too small for the modern jets like the Boeing 707, Douglas DC9s and Vickers VC10s. The new airport of Jorge Chavez International was opened near the port of Callao, 7 miles from Lima and 11 miles from where we lived in Miraflores. It meant that our days of watching all the aircraft taking off and landing were numbered as we seldom went all the way to Callao. But it never deterred me from my ambition, as I always wanted to be a pilot.

Yes, there were dangers living in this country. Diseases were the main concerns, especially after a particularly bad earth quake that would damage the sewerage system and the poor people's houses. We had around eight tremors a year, some mild, others violent. But you got used to them. Every year, Dr. Gonzales came to our house to give us all injections to immunize us from cholera, typhoid, malaria and yellow fever. These injections hurt and we were always very sore for weeks afterwards. I used to hide every time he came and when Mum and Juana caught me I had to be held down.

Apart from regular break-ins and robberies, we did have the very early days of the "Shining Path" terrorist group roaming around the country causing violent mayhem.

From a linguistic point of view, most of the time I spoke to my friends in Spanish or French, as this was the universally spoken tongue. When I turned eight, I had additional English lessons to learn how to read, write and speak in the language properly. I spoke with a Spanish guttural sound and often using a direct translation. I found English an illogical, back to front, complicated language – especially on spelling words and phrases which were pronounced the same but spelt differently. For instance:

"There and their; where and wear; or weather and whether" are three examples. "Dolor de la cabeza" directly translated is a pain of the head, but in English it's simply "a headache!??"

And as for this: "Ether, Either, neither, nor" what's all that about?

The rhyming chant we had to learn off by heart was: 'i' before 'e' except after 'c' if the sound is 'ee' but I still got confused on spelling received and reprieve. I still get it wrong!!

Little did I know that our parents were preparing me for something bigger a few years later in my early life.

You get the picture? I was living in a dream country, with a dream lifestyle and had lots of freedom and good fun.

Some people would not take to it or like the humidity or heat, nor the insects and the threat of earth tremors during the season. But for me ... I loved it!

CHAPTER TWO
UPHEAVAL

Dad came home one day in June and asked that Harriet and I be available at seven as he and mother needed to speak to us. He arrived home from work and went to have a shower and change into his white tuxedo, and then had a cocktail prepared by Carlos. Mum was also dressed in a summer evening dress as they were due at an embassy party or some other event that happened nearly every night.

Harriet and I were summoned into the lounge where Mum and Dad were sat having their pre-dinner drinks.

Dad cleared his throat.

'Your mother and I have decided that for your own good, we are sending you both to England to attend boarding school. Harriet, you are going to St Silvia's on the Isle of White and Charles you are going to Drummond College in Cheltenham. You start in the Autumn term which is September.'

Harriet was excited, well she was nearly thirteen, and she already knew she was going as eight or ten of her friends from school in Lima were also going.

I was devastated. My whole world caved in. I

was ten years old and very happy with my current life in Lima. So why did I have to go half way around the world to this god forsaken country, just because that's where Mum and Dad came from.

Anyway … England … where the hell was that?

I looked at my Mum, she was in tears, I knew she didn't want this to happen.

I asked Dad why and he insisted it was the best education he could afford to give me, and I would benefit long term. Schools in England were far better that those in Peru.

That was it … no debate, no arguments, no petitions, no objections. His word was law, and I had to obey.

I went to the school library the next day and looked up England in some of the reference books. It was a tiny little island off the coast of France, and it looked horrible.

'Bloody hell!! … look at this,' I said to myself reading the information 'in winter it snows and rains and gets to 10 F and in the summer, it gets as hot as our winters here!' I was despondent. My school chums came into the library as well.

'What's up Charlie?' Clive asked.

'I am going to England for school in September, somewhere called Chal .ten ..ham. I don't want to go.'

Clive looked at me and said 'Carlos, Ben and I are going to a school in Can't ...er...bury, in the south. Just been told too.'

'Hell, so why can't I go to your school in Cant.... bury?' I exclaimed.

That night I waited at the front door for father to arrive home.

Before he even had time to sit down with his drink I tackled him.

'Papa, Clive, Carlos and Ben are all going to a school called King's in Cantberry. Why can't I go there too, with them?' I said in a whining voice.

Dad just sat looking at me. Mum came out and sat me on her lap. 'Look Charlie, you have to go through a vetting process to gain entry to these exclusive schools and yours is a much better school that King's. Plus, we didn't know they were going there, and it's too late to change now.'

'I don't want to go to this school. Why does Harriet get to choose her school with her friends and I don't, it's not fair'?

There was no reconsideration. That was that and

I had to grin and bear it.

The only good news was that we were all going to England by ship, on the Reina del Mar, which would take 28 days. And we would be meeting my grandmother for the first time as well as my aunts and uncles, plus Auntie Joan, who was my Mum's guardian, and would become mine, too.

The upheaval of leaving home was tremendous. Yes, I would return home every Christmas to spend two months here, but for the English summer months I would spend it with Auntie Joan at her house in London or at her cottage in the Forest of Dean. A FOREST!! That's like going to Iquitos in the jungle for two weeks. I wondered if the English forests had all the same creatures as we had in the jungle, now that would be fun.

My English was OK. I could read and write well enough, but my pronunciation was awful according to Father. He promised I would have something called 'electrocution' lessons. Sounded horrible but it helps you with saying words properly.

Father also brought home some pamphlets on my new school that had loads of pictures of the playing fields, the church, the houses and dormitories, and it even had a tuck shop and a swimming pool too. We would learn to play cricket, hockey and rugby. Well I already played hockey and cricket (which was a boring game); Harriet played hockey and lacrosse which was much more fun. Harriet's pamphlet showed sailing and fishing as her school was situated on this tiny island off the south coast of this other island called England. Her school looked much nicer than mine, and she was there with her best friends. I was a touch jealous!!

◆◆

One day in June a huge trunk arrived. It was enormous and very heavy, big enough for me to get into. Juana said it was for me to pack all my clothes and belongings into that I wanted to take to school. She was very tearful and so was I as she had been our nanny since I was born.

When Mum and Dad were out at one of their parties and Harriet was at a sleep over, I used to go up to the roof and sleep with Juanita and Consuelo...... Wow now! ... hey guys ... I know what you are thinking!! ... I was only 7 or 8 ... I was too scared to be on my own in my room.

They were a great family to be with as they had lots of fun and were always happy; they played loads of different games to pass the time with Carlos and Maria.

We started to pack my trunk in July so that it was ready to board the ship in Callao docks. Well, 'we' was Mum and Juanita, with me putting things on the bed that I wanted to go with me, and being rejected by both!! But as it was so cold in England I insisted on packing my Peruvian llama wool-lined slippers, my llama wool balaclava, and my poncho and gloves too. I was not going to be cold. What I did not realise was that in Peru – everyone wore them so you didn't look out of place, but in England!!!!

I was very sad and scared to be leaving my home and my country to go to this foreign land half way around the world.

I DID NOT WANT TO GO!

No one would listen to me. Everyone was of the impression that it was a wonderful opportunity to expand my education and become more of a man. But pure and simply I did not want to go. I loved it here in Lima; I loved my life, my home, my friends …. even school!

I was lying in bed with my belongings all packed and decided to do something about this. To be honest, I don't know why I decided to do this. It was a dramatic gesture in my eyes, and not totally sure what it would achieve, but I got it in my stubborn mind to do it. It was very early in the morning and no one was up. I snuck into the kitchen and rummaged around. Found this old bottle of linctus that Maria had thrown out, so I washed it. Back in my room, I wrote a note on the inside of a matchbox toy carton box. I rolled the message up, put it in a plastic food bag, and popped it into the bottle. Whilst rummaging I found a hard rubber cork that was used for olive oil and I hammered this into the neck if the bottle to make sure it was tight. The bottle was small so it fitted into my pocket and I waited until we were on board the ship to throw it overboard once at sea.

I suppose that I gradually came to accept that I would not win my argument about staying at home, so I started to accept the inevitable.

Carlos and Maria were sad to see us go and wept when we eventually left the house. The night before Juanita came into my room and told me a tale of great adventures, and that I too will meet new friends and explore a new country. In no time at all I will be home for the holidays and she, Carlos and Maria would be home. Consuelo was engaged to be married and would be with her new family by then. Juanita was the one that changed my mind.

So, we were all excited on the day we left, tinged with sadness, but as we boarded the Reina del Mar we discovered that we had a family suite on board, that had a small sitting room and two bedrooms, so I had to share the room with bunk beds with my sister. Mum and Dad had the room with the large bed.

Dad had been in Peru since 1947, so he was returning to meet his bosses at his company in Lincoln, where Grandma lived. Then we were going to London to get our school uniforms and other supplies, then finally we were taken to school, me first then Harriet. Mum and Dad were flying back on this new BOAC Vickers VC10 super jet via New York.

We set sail from the port of Callao in the third week of July arriving in England at the end of the second week in August – England's summer.

The Reina del Mar was a 20,000-ton passenger liner of the PSNC company (Pacific Steam Navigation Company) built in 1950 by Vickers-Armstrong. It was

561 feet long and 73 feet wide, had a crew of 250 and carried 414 passengers and it was white everywhere with a single funnel. Dad was interested as it was propelled by two of his steam turbine engines. It was my first trip on a large ship and the 28-day voyage would take us through the Panama Canal to Montego Bay, Jamaica, then to Miami before crossing the Atlantic Ocean to England, arriving at somewhere called Liverpool. It was a fantastic ship, with a swimming pool and several restaurants where we could eat anything we wanted. We had full freedom to explore the ship, and I hooked up with two other boys who were also returning to the UK from Chile.

The ship was awesome, with so much to do every day. They had different clubs on board for everyone to participate in and Harriet and I with our new founds friends joined these clubs on deck, in the pool or in the theatre. It was educational as we learnt so much. We were fortunate that the ship wasn't full and the service was first class. The ships entertainment crew were pleased that the kids were so keen on playing with them. Besides some of the adults were a pain in the ass, always complaining about everything.

On the first morning at sea, I snuck out of my bunk bed and went up to the top deck with my message bottle. I threw it with all my strength out to sea and thought about where it would end up and who would find it. I told nobody about it as it was my one and only secret.

It took a week to get to Panama and the canal. Being pulled through the locks by the mechanical donkeys was fascinating, so we spent virtually all day at the ships railing on the top deck watching the workings and passage through the canal.

The next stop was Montego Bay, where we docked for three days to take on board provisions, and it gave us the opportunity to visit some of Jamaica. Mum and Dad took us to Ocho Rios to raft down the river and visit the Haunted House.

New passengers also joined the ship here, and it was the first time I met Chris Wrigley, who happened to be going to my school as well, and it was the start of a solid relationship. We were best friends by the time we docked in Liverpool.

Chris and I had very similar outlooks and tastes and it would turn out that we would support each other over the five years we were at school.

Halfway across the sea to Miami we hit a tropical storm, and everything was bolted down to the floor. Us kids spent the storm in the bowling alley, playing the rolly-poly game. We invented it for the journey; so basically, we would place our arms inside our T shirts so they were secured at our sides, and we would lie on the floor straight, playing dead, and as the ship pitched up we would roll down the bowling green, and when it pitched down we would roll back. The trick was to stay on the green stretch of the bowling alley and not fall out. We squealed with laughter, well the girls just squealed. None of us were sea sick, apart from the adults, but the storm lasted about eight hours.

Miami was another three days' stopover and we went to the Everglades and had trips on the aero boats, which was exhilarating and a bit scary too. Always at the back of your mind was falling off into the swamp and being eaten by an alligator. So, you didn't need to be told to hold on tight!

We went down the coast to Key West in a pale blue Cadillac that Dad had hired to see the beaches and the huge Naval base, but everyone was in mourning for Ernest Hemingway, the famous author, who had died on 2nd July. He was a huge figure in society here, as he lived most of his life in Key West.

We also visited the then very famous Daytona Beach, and whilst Mum and Harriet went to the beach, Dad and I went to the famous race track to watch the stock cars and the time trials on that day.

Unfortunately, Disney World in Orlando was still only an idea on the drawing board, although Walt Disney himself was in Florida negotiating the land deal that would eventually build the most impressive kids fun park in the world.

If we thought the storm between Jamaica and Miami was bad, the one we hit mid-Atlantic was ten times worse … and we were all sea sick this time. We were banned from playing any rolly-poly games as our parents and the crew feared one of us would get injured, and so were confined to our bunk beds for our own safety. The storm raged for a day and a night and it was the most frightening experience I have ever had. The gale force winds whipped up frightening twenty-foot waves, which crashed down on the decks and tossed the Reina del Mar about like driftwood. The ship rolled to port and starboard and climbed up one wave mountain and crashed down the other side. It was like "seabatics" – the sailing version of "aerobatics". Food was not an option as the chef in the galley would not light the stoves for risk of fire. We were offered cold sandwiches and lemonade, but we all felt too sick to eat anything.

The storm passed eventually and the ship regained service as normal. We were told that in a few hours we could see the headland which was the coast of Ireland, which we would pass on our way up the Irish Sea to Liverpool. We had been at sea for 30 days when we finally docked. Bearing in mind we were told that August was peak summer, the day we docked was dull and overcast and it was freezing cold. I had to wear a cardigan ... well it was 68F(20c) and to us that was cold, like winter in Lima.

Harriett, Chris the other kids and I watched the ship slowly make its way into port, helped by three tugs. It was very precise and we eventually tied up alongside a quay with a hive of activity. All the cars looked small and funny, the lorries and trucks were half the size of the American ones in Lima. Liverpool from the raised advantage of our deck height looked cramped and small. We were called to stand in a queue to disembark and our trunks and cases were taken by porters onto hand-pulled trolleys, which we had to open for the strange looking rotund custom man sweating under his official uniform cap. He was very officious and asked Dad loads of questions, looking at me as if I was a rare breed of ape. When the penny clicked later after hearing some comments made by people on the train, I realised why I or we looked strange. Although born 'white', being out in a hot climate does enhance a nice colour of your skin and I suppose to the ordinary British, we did look foreign. It would come home to me later that winter when I was undressing for a bath and looked at myself in the mirror and had a real fright. I went to Matron and told her I had a disease of some kind as my skin had all gone white. I was told in no uncertain terms not to be a "stupid boy" and sent back to my dorm with my backside tanned. I told everyone 'the man, he is like snake; we shed our skins'.

After, disembarking and going through customs, we said our goodbyes to everyone, and I told Chris we would meet again at school. At least there was one boy I would know

there. We were taken by cab to Liverpool Street railway station to catch a train to Lincoln. The train was a steam locomotive and Dad took me to the front of the platform to look at it. It was very small compared to the ones in Peru. The carriage had a long corridor off which were individual compartments with a sliding door. The seats were bench type with a luggage rack overhead. We settled down for the next part of our journey that would take all day. I sat and watched the countryside slide by. WOW .... this country was very, very green, and there were loads of animals in the fields. Cows, bulls, sheep, pigs and horses. I didn't see one llama or alpaca, and mum said that they didn't exist here in England. How strange was that?

All the cities and towns we went through were tiny. The

houses were very strange as they had funny hats on top, like 'V' shaped roofs, which you could not go onto. So where did all the house staff live then? I was fascinated by such differences. My mind was focusing on the fact that we were on a small island and therefore everything had to fit in.

'Papa, are all the cars, and trucks and houses smaller because they all have to fit into a small island?'

Dad was confused at first then the penny dropped.

'No Charlie, it's just that in England and Europe, they design everything differently from the Americans, and everything is smaller and neater, and in fact more efficient. It is why my company is so successful in South America, because it produces the best engines in the world. The American way is always bigger, and sadly as the USA is closer to us in Lima than England we get most of our goods from them.'

This baffled me totally and it took me several years to understand. Then when I went home one Christmas the difference in size came home to me.

◆◆

We arrived in Lincoln – finally, after going through about twenty stations along the route and changing trains twice, once in Leeds and once in Doncaster. Dad hailed a taxi to take our bags and trunks to Grandma's house although she only lived a stone's throw from the station. My first experience in an English house, and I held my breath as we went in. Grandma Grace hugged us and asked why I was holding my breath. 'Because your house is so small I don't want to use all the air in it;' 10-year-old logic. Everyone laughed at this except for Harriet who called me a moron.

Grandma's house was very small and in my view, it was only half a house, as it had two front doors.

The other half was owned by someone else. This to me was strange. Inside the house, it was very cramped and she had a lot of old furniture, the floors were even covered in carpet from wall to wall …. where did all the insects go? Her kitchen was long and narrow and she had a toilet outside in the backyard! She had three bedrooms, so we were crammed in and I had to sleep with Harriet in a small double bed. Grandma Grace was a lovely woman, she was Dad's mum and she was very tall with grey hair and she wore two cardigans and woolen socks. But she had small whiskers on her chin and lips which tickled when she kissed you.

We spent a week in Lincoln and again we met Dad's two sisters and their family. We went around the castle, and cathedral where Dad used to sing in the choir as a schoolboy; we also saw his school. We had a guided tour of Dad's engineering company, where we were taken around the foundry and assembly lines where they made the engines. This was a huge factory with a blast furnace where they made metal castings for the engine blocks! Dad told us that this is where our grandfather, his dad and his brother Frank used to work too, but sadly they both died some time ago.

In no time at all we were soon back on another

train heading for London, the capital city of England. We stayed in a small hotel off the Bayswater Road, and went sightseeing again. We visited the Tower of London and Tower Bridge, St Paul's Cathedral, the Houses of Parliament and several old museums. The best one was Madame Tussaud's where we saw lifelike waxworks of all the famous people. It was awesome. We went to see where the Queen lived and she had a really big house; bigger than the President's Palace in Lima. This was the first time I saw a palace bigger than those at home.

The plan was to collect all our school clothing from a department store called Gamages, which specialised in private school uniforms. Harriet went off with Mum to get hers in the girl's floor at a store called Harrods and Dad stayed with me for mine. My uniform consisted of a white cotton shirt with a maroon tie with the school coat of arms on it short grey flannel trousers, a maroon blazer, again with the school badge on it. We had long grey socks and sandal type shoes for the summer and black brogue shoes for the winter. It felt heavy and itchy, as in Lima we wore light and airy clothes for school. Dad ordered three pairs of everything, plus underwear and more socks. I had my swimming trunks and hankies etc.; from home. All the clothes were sent directly to the school as was my trunk from Lincoln. I had one uniform set with me to wear on my first day at school.

London was amazing, but again I thought everything was in miniature, the buses were all red and two stories' some with open-top upper decks. All the phone boxes, post boxes and many doors were also red. Was this a national colour?

All the soldiers were neater in their red uniforms, and the police were in dark blue, much classier than the khaki uniforms of the Peruvian army and police.

After a week in London, it was time to head for Cheltenham and my eventual incarceration into this prison of a school. Dad had hired a car to take us there as they had to drive to Harriet's school after dropping me off. Again, I was transfixed by the beauty of the countryside and how green everything was. The drive took virtually all day, but we did stop off for lunch and then tea and cakes on the way. We went through this place called Oxford, and Dad showed us one of the Universities and said that if I did well at school and got all the grades I could go here to get a degree, something he always wanted to do. I hated the thought as it looked very, very old and so spread out. All the students were forced to wear silly square hats and long, coloured gowns. I decided that I wouldn't like this. There were two major universities in England at Oxford and Cambridge, and everyone aspired to finish their education at these places. Well to me it looked all too serious and not much fun at all.

As we had plenty of time before we were due at my new school, Dad took a small detour through a pretty little town called Moreton-in-Marsh where we had lunch in a restaurant in the main high street, and then we stopped off for tea at a little village called Broadway, which had sentimental memories for Mum and Dad, during their courtship. The little tea shop had delicious cakes which I devoured.

Harriet and Mum went off shopping again and Dad and I just sat in the sunshine finishing off our tea. Dad wanted to have some time with me.

'Charlie, you know why Mum and I want you to enjoy Drummond College, don't you?' he said looking at me.

'Well it's a great privilege and I wish I had this opportunity to have such a good start in life. I have learnt that a good education will take you a very long way and I never had that. I had to work very hard to get my engineering degree and if I had a leg up like this I would have found life a lot easier.'

I was listening but didn't quite understand what he was getting at. All I could see was that they were dumping me at a strange school eight thousand miles from my home and friends, in a foreign country that was freezing bloody cold; everywhere was small and they all spoke with funny accents. All this talk about getting a better education, why couldn't we get this at home?

Harriet was laughing as she had all her school friends with her at her school. So unfair!

In fact, little did I know that my education at Drummond College would be more than just primary lessons, and that I would learn a good few facts about life and how to survive in a hostile environment.

And yes .... it did set me up for life.

CHAPTER THREE
AND SO TO SCHOOL

Drummond College was housed in two huge four story houses, probably built in the early 1900s. When we arrived after our circumnavigation of the English countryside, we were greeted by the Headmaster Mr. Langhorne, who was an incredibly tall, skinny man with huge glasses. He had bulbous eyes, a long straight nose and mickey mouse ears with an Adam's apple that bounced up and down when he talked. We were introduced to 'Matron' Mrs. Ramsbottom, who oversaw all the catering, nursing and administration staff. She would supervise bedtime and everything to do with our health and hygiene, she was a large, rotund lady with a huge bosom and a massive rear, in her fifties and wore a nurse's uniform. She had dark facial hair and was frightening to a young 10-year-old boy.

Mum, Dad, Harriet and I were given a tour of the school, looking at classrooms, the science lab, the dining hall and kitchens, the gym, playing fields, tuck shop, swimming pool and finally our dormitories. Here there would be seven to a room, headed by a Dorm Prefect.

41

The Head Boy and his five deputies had their own rooms, and we met a few of them, but there was so much to take in we didn't really talk to them.

Mum and Dad said a long goodbye, Mum especially was in tears and would not let go of me. It was heart-breaking to watch them go with Harriet.

The one thing that distracted me was the arrival of Chris Wrigley, and especially when we found out we were in the same dorm and next to each other as well.

In the dorms, we had a single hard bed with a bedside table and our trunks under the bed with all our clothes in it.

We were told to settle in and meet everyone in the dining hall for assembly before the evening meal.

All the new boys assembled together with the dorm prefects who were 2nd or 3rd year students, and the Head Boy and deputies. All the teachers were there as well, and the Head addressed us all welcoming us to the school.

He then outlined all the rules of the school, which is when I discovered this ritual called 'fagging'. This is the abhorrent tradition of breaking in a new boy into subservient life, by making him a 'servant' to a prefect or one of the deputy head boys. I suppose the army has a similar position. Your duties were to make the prefects bed in the morning, clean his shoes, take his clothes to the launderette to be cleaned and running errands at the boy's will. It also required the boy to clean the grate of the fire in the Head Boy's study and remake the fire every morning before breakfast, whether it was still hot or not. I was not having this!

'Dashwood, you are to fag for Ames,' the Head Boy said to me poking me with his whipping cane.

Oh yes ... each deputy and prefect had little whipping canes which they were allowed to use to give light punishment for unruly boys.

'No. Ees no possible,' I replied in my pigeon English with guttural accents. The letter 'H' comes out as if you have something stuck in your throat ... a sort of jch sound 'I jchave staff at my house in Lima. I am no staff jchere,' I stood very defiant and slightly haughty.

The Head Boy strides up to me and comes within an inch of my nose and shouts at me, 'WHAT?' Spittle spreads over my face. 'WHAT DID YOU SAY, Dashwood?' And with that raises his cane to strike me. I grab the cane on its downward path and hold his stare. I have always been very tall for my age, and even though he was five years older I was still level with his face. I am sure that this added to his wrath.

I stand up a bit taller and reply equally strongly,

'I say to you NO. I NO DO THIS.'

Head Boy was shaking with anger. The Headmaster and other teachers watched this but did not interfere.

Head Boy still faces me, 'you are a little insignificant wop. You come to our school and defy hundreds of years of tradition and expect ME to accept this. You are going to be trouble Dashwood and I am going to take personal interest in you. Now you WILL DO AS YOU ARE TOLD, and NEVER, NEVER dare touch my cane again.'

I then grab his cane out of his hand and look at it. Then throw it on the floor.

'PICK THAT UP DASHWOOD – NOW,' he screams.

The whole room is deadly quiet, I don't think they have ever had a junior boy, let alone a newbie on their first day, be as defiant as this.

I stand very still and look at him 'NO, YOU DO THIS NO ME.'

With this the Headmaster steps in to diffuse the

situation. 'Dashwood, I want you in my study in an hour. I think we need to have a little chat about rules at this school. Ames and Worrall (the Head Boy) I want you to wait outside my office until I call you in.'

The other ten new boys are allocated to the dorm prefects or the deputies without any further trouble. But I notice that four other boys were different from the others, one being Chris Wrigley.

Drummond College was one of the top ten public schools in England, and therefore it was a privilege to be here. In the main the pupils came from families who were either in the armed forces, foreign office diplomats, or aristocracy, all high-end families, all very arrogant people as they thought they were superior. There was a handful of pupils whose parents worked overseas for British commercial companies like me. In the 1960s to 1970s in public schools in the UK, corporal punishment was legal and a way of punishment for errant schoolboys. At our school, they also empowered the Head Boy, his deputies and prefects to use small whipping canes to keep order and punish small offences.

♦♦

I was soon to meet my fellow friends, as Matron had decided for political reasons to house us all together in one dormitory. We were taken upstairs to our room and then left to unpack and settle in.

'Dashwood, don't forget Headmaster wants to see you in half an hour,' she said as she left us alone.

I look at my fellow friends. Chris comes up to me and shakes my hand.

'That took guts,' he said.

The next boy came up to me and then we all introduced each other, shaking hands.

Tobias Mortimer was from the USA - Texas. His family owned a very large cattle ranch and he had a lovely American drawl to his voice. His greeting was always 'Hi yawl.'

Kando Oboke was from N'dola in Africa. He lived in Nigeria and his father owned a business there. He was very black and taller and broader than me, he would become our protector as no one would take him on in a fight.

Titus la Croix was from French Guyana and his parents were from a wealthy fashion industry background.

And of course, Chris Wrigley from St Kitts in the

Caribbean.

We became known as the famous five or "the gang of five" and little did we realise the bond we would have over the next five years.

There were two other boys in our dorm plus the dorm prefect made eight in our dorm.

I was taken to the Headmaster's study in the big house next door. It was a very large dark room, with a thick dark red carpet, a huge square desk in one corner, and most of the main floor of the room was clear of furniture. There were four chairs next to his desk, and a wooden rack full of different sized canes and walking sticks. The walls were lined with framed pictures of past schoolboys from every year. There were hundreds of them covering two of the walls. There were two bay windows looking out to the playing fields framed by heavy maroon curtains. The room smelled of old books and stale air. His desk was littered with papers and books and he had a brass desk lamp that was switched on.

We knocked at his door and waited. The Head Boy and prefect were already stood outside waiting and they gave me a hard stare when I looked at them.

'Come Dashwood,' his deep booming voice came from the other side.

We walk in and I am told to stand in the middle of the room. The teacher who brought me left the room.

The Headmaster was sat at his desk reading a paper. He slowly looks up at me and removed his glasses. He sat quietly contemplating with the arm of his spectacles in the corner of his mouth. He cleared his throat.

'Dashwood, I am going to make allowances for you this time. I know you have servants at home as do most of the boys here. They all come here as their parents are overseas either in the armed forces or as your parents, working for UK companies,' he paused to see if I was understanding him.

'This school is coming up to one hundred-years-old, and whether we like it or not, we have traditions to keep and are ruled by, through the governance of the school rules. And so, I am aided and supported by a team outside the teaching staff, made up of senior boys who have all gone through the initiation stages you are about to go through. The Head Boy has earnt his position, because he is the best boy at this school in everything he does, both scholastically as well as physically, as have all his deputies. The dorm prefects are chosen by him and they have a duty to perform too. They hold discipline as well as guidance to all the new boys. They have my authority to use their directional canes to give light punishment if a boy consistently strays. What I am trying to explain to you is that you cannot buck the system. You should accept our ways and work with us. I understand that fagging seems demeaning to you, but you should do it for at least a year or until new boys arrive. I am going to ask you to work with us. You will find out that by doing so your passage through the initial months here will be smoother.'

He then picked up a letter and re-read it again before continuing.

'Your father wants the best for you and states that you are a headstrong boy. Your understanding of English is good I understand, but your speech needs some help. You are to receive additional elocution lessons from Mrs. Yates. Now before I call Head Boy in, is there anything you wish to say?'

I looked at the Headmaster and thought about a response. My mind was racing. Do I submit to this fagging or do I continue to resist?

'Is good now Senior Langhorne. I no like being

servant, but will be ok, if they no shout at me.'

He smiled at me, then shouted 'Worrall and Ames, come.'

There was a knock at the door and in came the Head Boy and Ames. They came and stood next to me quite still.

'Now Worrall and Ames. Dashwood and I have spoken and he will agree to his duties to you Ames, but don't push him. We must respect his culture and his work with his level of understanding English language. I feel confident that you will show him the ropes and get him settled in without any need for persuasions. Go now.'

And the interview was finished.

Outside the Head's office, Worrall looked at me, then said to Ames 'He's all yours Ames – take him back to dorms and then to supper.'

Then to me, 'behave Dashwood and you will do OK.'

The gang of five were waiting for me to return to find out what happened. Ames said he would go through my duties tomorrow morning after prayers.

Oh yes … the school had its own church and as a multi-cultural body we had prayers every morning at seven. Our typical day was followed by breakfast at eight and lessons started at nine until twelve thirty. Lunch was served; then we had free time until two when we had more lessons until three thirty in the summer followed by games – cricket and running. In the winter, the games started at two when we played rugby and hockey. They had a swimming pool which we used after games and before prayers at six, supper at seven and study period until nine when it was lights out by nine thirty.

◆◆

Our first night's sleep was strange as I had never had to share with eight boys before. Even when we went camping up in the Cordillera mountains in Peru, we were only four to a tent. I didn't sleep well at all that first night, my head spinning with all that I had experienced so far. Why am I here, I kept on asking myself? I had a gut feeling that it was going to get worse.

Next morning at six a bell rang waking us all up. Ames was already up and dressed telling us to get showered and into our school uniform.

We were led in single file out of our 'house' and

over the fields to the church for the 30-minute service of morning prayers and hymns. This was followed by breakfast in the refectory or dining room.

The dining room was a huge room with eight long wooden tables with long trestle seats either side. The Headmaster and teachers ate with the Head Boy and deputies on their own table. We were called up by our dorm numbers for self-service, and I loved breakfast as it had delicious food. Sausages, bacon, baked beans, doorstep fried bread and eggs. Oh …. and loads of toast, butter and my favourite – marmalade. When we had all finished – if there was any food left - we could help ourselves and I discovered the delicious combination of cold fried bread with a thick layer of marmalade spread over the top.

When the other schoolboys found out I came from Peru, I got the nickname "Paddington" – especially for my love of marmalade … how original!!

◆◆

There were the bully boys, who thought they were above the law. These were a small group of 3rd years who had been passed over for either dorm prefect or deputies, but thought they were due some sort of privileges from the lower forms, and decided to push their weight around. They were often caught by the Head Boy or his deputies and they were punished and they were not that bright. It was my very first lesson in life, knowing that those who abuse others, are personally weak and feeble characters who hide behind this façade of the 'tough boy act'. We were an ideal target for them as we were "different" from the other boys. And they would push us deliberately in assembly or when we were standing chatting; or demand and take sweets we had bought at the school tuck-shop. Sometimes we were beaten up if found on our own, so the gang of five kept together most of the time.

The way the school worked was that the dorm of seven kept together and we all had the same lessons as well. We were given a timetable of lessons held in the classrooms on the ground or basement floors of both houses. Over the coming months, I found that my favourite subjects were, French (Mademoiselle Fabien – was a late twenty-something French single very attractive brunette, and all the boys lusted after her);

Geography, English and Religious Education. My worst subjects were Maths, Greek and Latin; Physics and Chemistry.

Mr. Rowland was the math's teacher, and he was a tall gangling man made of rubber. He had a huge head with a massive beaked nose, stick out ears, large round glasses, and a black moustache which he greased. He was a hot shot chalk thrower, as if you didn't pay attention he would throw the chalk in his hand with such force and accuracy that it stung when it hit you on the cheek or hand. Occasionally – if he was really fed up with you - he would hurl the blackboard rubber at you then make you stand on a chair in the corner of the room for the whole lesson. No wonder my maths is still my worst subject.

The other teachers were all very nice and patient especially the Greek and Latin teacher who had an uphill struggle with us as we thought there was no point in learning dead languages, until we discovered that Spanish, French, Italian and English were derived from Latin. This made it partly interesting.

Three nights a week or sometimes at lunch break or on Sundays I would have elocution lessons with Mrs. Yates, who taught me how to speak the Queen's English and helped round my pronunciations and in three years she eliminated my Spanish accent. One of her tricks was to roll dried hard peas into cotton wool and place these inside the cheeks of my mouth, and made me say some rhymes such as, "How now brown cow" or "Hallowed hills hold hollow holes," and these were repeated over and over, each time pronouncing the words perfectly. I liked her as she was nice.

Then we all had deportment lessons with Matron and the Headmaster, who taught us how to lay a table for a formal evening dinner, which piece of cutlery to use, what it was for and in which order to use them (outside to inside). They taught us how to sit properly with our bums tucked into the back of the chair, and our backs ramrod straight; how to cross our legs and then how to walk, with straight backs carrying books on our heads to keep the stance straight. And finally, we had lessons in decorum, what to call and how to address people of rank, when to speak and when not to speak to elders and seniors, and holding doors open for ladies, plus loads more.

◆◆

On day two the food trouble started. As I walked into the refectory, I was hit by the most revolting smell I had ever had. Now I was used to going through the shanty towns in Lima and the horrid smell of decay and putrid sewerage enhanced by humidity and a very hot climate, but this … it was much worse. I was told it was cook boiling cabbage and Brussels sprouts. How disgusting. We had chicken, or beef, or ham with Brussels, cabbage and swede. These revolting vegetables don't exist in Peru – thank god! – and they tasted like sick. So, I refused to eat them.

Well that started yet another ruckus.

First Matron came over and told me to eat it. Then cook came out and asked what was wrong with it.

'Eete is no nice. Smell bad, taste bad; I no eat.'

'But it's good for you so you have to eat it.'

'NO … I no eat. Why you not cook rice or papas, or noodle … that is good for you, no this sheet.'

WHACK came a hand right across my face. Cook stood there shaking.

'He called my food shit,' she said and the whole room giggled with laughter.

'BE QUIET ALL OF YOU;' bellowed the Headmaster.'

He came up to me and leaned into my face.

'Now Dashwood, what's all the commotion about this time. You seem to be a nuisance and have only just arrived here. I hope this is not an onerous sign?'

'Senior, dis food eet is nota nice. Eet smell make me sickly. I no eet dis food.'

'Well I am afraid you will have to grin and bear it Dashwood as we are not going to prepare special diets for you.'

The Headmaster had a grin on his long face and his "Adams" apple bounced up and down as if he was chuckling to himself. 'Settle down everyone,' said the head and turning to Matron, 'I think Dashwood may need some help in eating our food Matron. You know what to do.'

I was made to sit at the refectory table with a deputy either side of me and Matron, spoon in hand, was force feeding me this revolting food. I was choking with every mouthful, and on the third I spat it out, stood up and said

'No more. I no eat no more,' And then sat with my mouth firmly shut and arms folded across my chest. They didn't know what to do with me, so let me go to my dorm to wash and change as I had mushed cabbage and swede all round my face and down my shirt.

I soon discovered the art of sleight of hand. With the help from the gang of five, they distracted Matron, the prefects and cook, whilst I stuffed my pockets with Brussels, cabbage and swede; then had to go all afternoon stinking of this until I could empty my pockets in the toilet and wash my shorts.

By March I had to write to Father asking permission to order another three pairs of shorts from Gamages, as my pocket linings were going rotten!

Please don't think that I was always awkward towards the food. I loved the meat pies, the chicken pies, the shepherd's pie, kippers and white fish and most of the food. We did have peas, runner beans, green beans, salad and sweetcorn from time to time and very occasionally, rice and pasta too. But in the main it was mashed potatoes, congealed mushed cabbage, Brussels and smelly mashed swede. (*to this day fifty years on, I still don't eat these three vegetables!*).

The gang and I used to break into the kitchens at night and make cheese and jam, or banana and Marmite sandwiches to take back to our rooms. Tobias suggested that to keep him sweet, we make one for Ames too so that he wouldn't rat on us. He very much liked this.

In fact, after three months Ames got to like us "foreigners" and loved to hear of all our tales from our different lifestyles at home. Especially Chris, Kando, Titus and I as we came from exotic countries. Although Tobias had some interesting stories from his ranch in Texas and Titus had an easy life with his two sisters living in French Guyana, but spending summer holidays in France on a vineyard with his uncle. After lights out we would all sit on Ames's bed and tell different stories of our escapades and what our countries were like. Kando had the hardest life in Africa, and Chris and I had similar lives, involving horse-riding, swimming and sailing and other adventures.

Ames's dad was a fighter pilot, a Squadron Leader in the Royal Navy Airforce on board an aircraft carrier somewhere in the Far East. His mom lived in Spain with another man, so he had a split home life. Later that year I started to teach Ames some Spanish so when he went home to Spain for Christmas he could surprise his Mum and her partner.

We did have a moment of excitement on one of our missions to the kitchens. Lights out at nine thirty, so we waited until nine fifty when Matron had done her rounds; when Chris and I sneaked out of the dorm through the big sash window and down the fire escape. We hugged the walls to avoid being seen in the open and went through the kitchen backdoor. As we crept quietly into the washing up and plate room, we heard a female giggling. It was coming from the kitchen itself which just had the blue fly trap lights on, but light enough to see.

There was Worrall, the Head Boy, with his trousers around his ankles, standing in between a girl's legs and doing a backward and forward movement. She was sat with her legs apart on the work surface and was leaning back on her elbows, with her head back, nearly touching the surface, panting like she had run a few miles. Worrall was sweating and making funny grunting noises as his rhythm increased. Chris and I, at ten years of age, had heard about this sex thing but never seen it, so it was our first introduction to voyeurism. Chris could not contain a snort, and leaned back into some pots and pans that made a crashing sound. Worrall froze and the girl said, 'Keep bloody going, don't stop now you tosser.'

Worrall shouted, 'Whose there?' But we dare not reveal ourselves, so we backed out of the rear door quickly and made our way back to the dorm via the fire escape. We jumped on our beds laughing and told the others and Ames what we had seen. Ames said it was one of cook's helpers in the kitchen, a local girl who obliged for a few shillings. He knew that Worrall was up to something but did not know what until now. This would come in useful later for both me and Ames. But no sandwiches for a midnight snack that night!

◆◆

As the winter progressed, I was introduced to a new phenomenon, that I had only seen at a distance in the mountains of Peru; snow and rain! Gosh it was bloody cold. I wore two vests under my shirt and two sweaters under my blazer. I had never felt rain before as it never rained in Peru on the coastal region, only high in the Andes or the Amazon Jungle.

We were forced to play games of rugby and hockey in the rain as well and I froze to death. It was cruel and so unkind, I thought.

One afternoon, after sports, I was in the showers cleaning off the mud on my own, and getting warm under the hot water, when two senior boys came in with towels wrapped around themselves, they had also just come in from games. They said:

'Well, well, well look what we have here, one of the Latin boys all on his lonesome. What, no friends today Paddington? What are we going to do Gary? Perhaps a little lesson in humility and some respect for senior boys. If you hold him, I will show him what we do to snivelling little first years.'

With that the leader of the two approached me and grabbed my willy in one hand and my ass with his other hand as his friend grabbed me from behind. Being taller than them, I pulled away and kicked him as hard as I could in the groin, then raised my elbow and swung round into the other boy's throat, and they both went down in the wet shower pan. I then lifted the leaders head up and with all my strength punched him in the face. I heard a crunch as my fist went through his teeth and he screamed in pain.

'Maybe you jchave some respect for us to, idiota,' I swore at him in Spanish, before walking out of the shower rooms to dry off and get changed.

Some of the prefects and deputies ran into the shower block to see what the commotion was about, and shouted for Matron and the PE Master. They asked if anyone knew what had happened, but we all kept quiet. The other boys knew it was me and I had to hide my bleeding knuckles wrapped in some toilet paper and my towel.

The boy had to go to hospital as I had broken his front teeth, and the other boy had a huge black bruise on his neck. There was an investigation, and the Head Boy asked me how I had injured my hand. I told him it was a hockey scrape, and he left it at that. Of course, the boys dare not report me, and they kept very silent as attempted rape of a first year was a serious offence that would have expelled them. Still my card was marked and I would be punished for this later.

A few weeks later we had our first introductions to swimming lessons, and the school PE teacher discovered that I could swim like a fish. In fact, Chris, Kando, Titus and I were all very strong swimmers, but I was the fastest having had all those private lessons in Peru from the German swimming teacher. I became swimming captain and represented the school at inter-school swimming competitions, which we tended to win. We swam naked in our pool, but had to wear trunks when there were parents or other schools present.

The swimming pool was the one place to get our own back on the bully boys, who struggled to swim. This is where we discovered their cowardice and we took full advantage of our upper hand every time we were rostered to swim with them. The PE teacher knew they were bullies and seemed to turn a blind eye, but making sure we didn't drown any of them! We would dive underneath and pull them down, holding them under until they swore not to bully us. Great fun!!

I also excelled at hockey, a sport I played in Peru, so I got into the first eleven playing for the school in my year. Cricket bored me and I could never understand why Dad loved to play this game at the Cricket Club in Lima.

The first Christmas I spent in England, I stayed with Aunt Joan; firstly, at her little cottage in Theydon Bois in Essex (she was a Professor of English language at London University, so would help me work on my grammar and pronunciation in holiday time) and Harriett went to a friend's house in Switzerland skiing – the lucky mare. Mum and Dad could not afford to come to the UK twice in one year, and promised that Harriet and I would go to Lima in November to January next year for the Christmas break. Aunt Joan was soon to retire from teaching and had bought a house in the Forest of Dean, somewhere called St Briavels which was in Monmouthshire and only an hour's drive from the school. Lucky me!!

I had survived the first three months at school without any caning or serious detentions, and I kept out of the Head Boys way as well as cook, and Matron.

The only time I got really ribbed was when I wore my Peruvian llama wool balaclava as it was multi coloured like the Indians wear up in the Andes. Together with my gloves and poncho I stood out a mile. Some of the deputies and teachers told me it wasn't school uniform and therefore I could not wear it, but I ignored them, telling them it was too cold in this country. I got called "The Boy from Peru" or "Paddington".

There was a brief time when I became ill and had

flu, so was isolated in the attic rooms that doubled as the school's medical wing. I was fed soup and toast and had the whole place to myself for the first few days, until more boys became infected and joined me in the attic.

◆◆

After returning from Christmas break, the next few months were gruelling as winter turned to spring and I slowly got used to the English weather. The summer brought prospects of a different timetable as the morning and evenings got lighter. Sports changed from rugby and hockey to cricket and cross country runs, although I still played the odd game of summer hockey in tournaments. We also had the option to start horseback riding at a stable just out of town. So, things started to look up a bit.

The gang of five all opted for cross country running and horse riding, and we were taken to the stables after being kitted out in jodhpurs and shirts.

There was this elegant lady and her daughter who ran the stables. She had a very plummy accent and was difficult to understand at first, but her daughter who was 13 and went to Cheltenham Ladies College, was better

and so nice too, she helped at weekends. Mrs.
'Partington-Smythe (or Mrs. 'P' as we came to call her)
stood on a small wooden crate and gathered us around
her.

'Hello boys. Now how many of you have ridden
horses before?' she asked. I put my hand up, as did
Titus, Chris and Tobias. Kando looked uncertain as he
had never seen a horse, zebra yes, but not ridden one!!'

'That's splendid, well we shall see what you can
do. Millicent, can you bring the horses out. You boy.'
pointing at Kando 'have you not ridden before?'

'No miss, only zebras,' he said with a smile on
his face; we all giggled, as did Millie, and when she
laughed, her face lit up.

'Harrumph,.' coughed Mrs. P, 'Ok this is not a
laughing matter. You will go with Suzie here to the
novice yard. The rest of you we will allocate horses to
you and go to the exercise field with Millie and I, and
we will see what you can do.'

Millicent brought out a huge 16 hand dark brown
Irish Hunter for me with this little piece of leather on its
back.

'Here you are. This is Paddy. I hope you like
boisterous horses, as he is a bit of a challenge,' she

smiled at me.

'Ees no problem. I jchave my jchorse at jchome too. Ees a palomino,' then I went around Paddy stroking his neck and nose and hind quarters as we got to know each other. I was being closely watched by Millie and her mum. I stood looking at the saddle, never seen one of these before. How were you supposed to sit on that, it was tiny, just like everything else in this country?

'Is there a problem?' Mrs. Partington-Smythe said to me.

'Yes, where ees de saddle. Dis is too small, I no ride with dees,' pointing at the saddle.

'I thought you said you can ride?' she asked. Millie came around and said to her mother, 'Mumsie he told me he had a Palomino back home.'

'Where is home Dashwood?'

'I came from Peru, and I can ride bare back and jchave a much beeger saddle dan dees one.'

Then it clicked, in South America, we have everything American and our saddles were the deep seats with high pommels and long stirrups and we sat to the trot.

'Oh, my god, we have two cowboys here,' said Mrs. 'P'.

Of course, Tobias was the same.

We spent our first three lessons learning to rise to the trot, with Mrs. 'P' shouting at us, 'rise Dashwood, rise Mortimer, you are not herding cows now.'

But after lessons, Millie would take us bareback riding across the fields, watched by her mum who was secretly impressed with Tobias and my skills on the horses. We always finished by brushing them down. This was one of the highlights of my school in England. I was to meet Millie later in different circumstances.

◆◆

Although school life was not boring, and we had plenty of activities, I longed for home, and got what is called 'home sickness'. Chris felt the same way and we were chatting one day about how easy it would be to escape from school, after the kitchen raids down the fire escapes gave us ideas. We looked at how we would get back home and we decided to do a project on this. We wrote to BOAC, and Air France, and we walked down to the railway station on our Sunday exeats and got timetables for trains to London. We wrote to London Airport (it was renamed Heathrow in 1966) saying we were doing a school project and wanted to know how bags and passengers were loaded onto planes and the inner workings of the airport. We got tube and bus timetables as well *(although the tube only went as far as Hatton Cross in those days – the extension to Heathrow was made in the 70s)*. This took about six months to gather all the information. However, we kept it a secret from the others as we knew how word got around the school, and we hid all our information books in our trunks under our beds.

One day in August, Chris said to me, I think it is probably better if we cross the playing fields and hitch a ride with a truck driver going to London, instead of the train. We agreed to try it out. We packed a small duffel bag with some clothes and our pocket money, and hid our big coats under the beds.

We waited until everyone was in bed before we got dressed into our school uniforms and got under the covers waiting until after lights out. When everyone was asleep we slipped onto the landing and out through the fire escape.

We kept to the borders of the playing fields and down to the main road. We saw the signs for Reading on the A436 and headed up that road. It was very dark by this time and as a country road it had no street lights nor pavements, but there was a full moon and the sky was clear so we had relatively good lighting to see where we were going. We seemed to walk for hours and it was all uphill. Eventually we saw bright lights in the distance and headed for these. It was the Air Balloon Pub on a roundabout, and there was plenty of cars and lorries driving slowly by.

We stopped just across the road near a layby, and a huge tanker lorry pulled up and stopped in the middle of the road. The driver got out and asked if we were lost. We asked him if he was going to London, and would he give us a lift. He readily agreed, and told us to hop into the lorry. We both climbed up the steep steps into the cab and settled into the seats. The driver said he needed the toilet, and parked the lorry up in a layby just opposite the pub. He went off and we waited for him.

After about twenty minutes we saw blue flashing lights appear and three police cars arrived; one pulled up in front of the lorry, one behind and one into the pub car park. The driver had heard on his CB radio that two boys were missing from the local school and when he saw Chris and I he surmised correctly it was us!

The police put us in the back seats of one of the cars to take us back to school, telling us how much trouble we were in. We asked them if they would put the siren and lights on, but they only put the lights on, as it was too late at night for the siren.

When we arrived back at school, all the lights were on in both the houses, and the Headmaster, Head Boy, Matron, Ames and a few others were there waiting for us at the main entrance steps. The Headmaster's face looked like thunder, and Matron had her arms crossed. Not a good sign.

'Now you two escapees, go to your dormitory with Ames and I will see you in my study at eight tomorrow morning,' Mr. Langhorne said to us in a very serious voice. We hear clapping and hurrahs from our dorm window as the rest of the gang welcomed us back.

The next morning the Head Boy came into our room at seven thirty. He was holding his cane in one hand and gently hitting his other with the tip. 'You boys are in very serious trouble. We have never had any boys escape before and Mr. Langhorne is very worried about you. I hope you have a bloody good excuse.'

We were marched across to his study, knocked on the door and entered when called. In the study was

Matron and the deputy head.

He was silent for a while, appraising us carefully by looking at us up and down. He cleared his throat.

'Never, in the history of this school, have we ever had one pupil, let alone two attempt an escape. It brings humiliation and disgrace to our school. We will be the laughing stock of the top public schools in this country. What you boys have done is severe enough to be expelled. We cannot reach your parents, so we have decided that we will give you a second chance. Now before I hand out your punishments, please explain yourselves.'

Chris started 'It was my fault Headmaster. I encouraged Dashwood to come with me. We just wanted to go home and see our families. We don't like it here, especially what happed to Dashwood in the showers,' he bleated out.

I looked at Chris and frowned at him. He was not supposed to say anything about that. I needed to deflect this.

'No Senior. Eet was my fault. I no speak good English. I ask my friend Wrigley to come with me and, Si, we wanted to go jchome.'

'What's this about the showers Dashwood,' he

asked.

I kept silent, but Chris wanted to defend me 'two seniors tried to rape Dashwood in the showers a few months back and he had to defend himself.'

'So that's why you had a bandaged hand,' said the Head Boy.

'They no trouble me again. They are disgusting boys so I jchad to fight with them off me,' I said in defence.

Matron took a sharp intake of breath, as the deputy head just tutted and shook his head.

The Headmaster stroked his chin in contemplation. Finally, he reaches into his collection of canes and selected a long thin one.

'Your punishment for running away will be 12 of the best across your backsides. I would have made it more but for clearing up the beatings has been a mystery to us and you should not have been subjected to that ordeal. I do not condone you actions in fighting with them, but I will accept that it was self-defence on this occasion. However, running away is an altogether different issue and for this I am going to have to discipline you. So, both of you … trousers down and bend over holding your ankles tightly.'

We both took our turns as the Headmaster aimed the cane across our buttocks and brought the cane down on us with some force. It stung like mad. Neither of us could sit down for a week, despite Matron applying iodine and bandages.

Eleven years old and we were famous. The next day we were in all the local papers and one national. The Headmaster was trying desperately to dumb it down and told reporters to get off private property. It goes without saying that Ames also had the cane for not supervising us sufficiently, and the Head Boy also had a serious talking to by the Head as well.

Around the school we became infamous, and everyone treated us with respect and reverence, even the deputies and other prefects. To have the guts, the nous and determination to plan and execute such an escape was awesome.

However, our parents didn't think so, and a week later I received a letter from Father describing his anger at my selfishness, and that we would be discussing this when I came home for Christmas.

Our other punishment was withdrawal of tuck shop rights, and they stopped us from horse-riding for the rest of the term. We were watched all the time, which meant I had to eat some of the cabbage, Brussels and swede, as Matron and the other prefects followed us everywhere.

The following week, we got the news which spread throughout the school that two boys had been expelled for lewd behaviour. These were the two boys who attacked me in the showers. Good riddance.

Chris and I had the chance to discuss the failed plan the following month and decided that when we went home next time, we would make loads of notes and take pictures on Chris's new Kodak camera of every part of the journey, so we could be better prepared for the second attempt.

We had to admit that it was very exciting and worth every stroke of the cane. In one of my letters home, I asked Mum and Dad if I could have a camera as a joint Christmas and birthday present.

The next few months passed by with very little excitement, apart from the Head Boy trying to blackmail us for information on Ames, who had become a good friend to the gang of five. We were inseparable, and defended each other from bullies and other attempts to frame us for the many different activities that other boys got up to.

One evening Worrall caught Chris and I in the library and shut the door. He tapped his cane on his shin and started to ask us in a very threatening tone, what Ames was doing.

We told him to back off and leave us and Ames alone.

'What are you saying Dashwood?' He leered at me, 'are you threatening me because that would be a very unwise tact to take old boy?'

I looked him square in the eye …. we were of the same height. My elocution lessons were paying off as I had softened the 'H' now and could imitate the posh speaking plummy mouthed boys.

'How is Mary, the kitchen maid? Does the stainless-steel tops of the kitchen hurt your willy, or her bum?' Chris sniggered.

He blushed and said with a hiss, 'If you ever dare to breathe a word of this you will be in very deep trouble.'

We had the upper hand, so I stood up to him and said, 'you cover our backs now, or you will be in even deeper trouble.'

CHAPTER FOUR
HOME FOR CHRISTMAS

Before we broke up for Christmas; many of us were travelling overseas to go home to see our parents, some to India, some to the Far East and others to Australia; and of course, Chris, Titus and Tobias were flying west; so, in our last geography session, the teacher spent a whole lesson on time zones, seasons, and health. We learnt for instance that if you travelled west from UK you lost time and if you travelled east you gained time. Kando was only an hour ahead to Lagos. St Kitts and Lima were in the same time zone and they were -5 hours behind London, whereas Sidney in Australia was +10 in front.

I was starting to get collywobbles in my stomach. The next few days would be awesome as this was my first real flight in a big jet and I was just so excited.

And so, it was that we started planning our escape the day that Chris Wriggly and I got on the train at Lansdowne Road railway station to London at eight thirty that morning, then catching the flight from Heathrow at four thirty in the afternoon via Paris, back home. We had this crazy notion that we could sneak on board the BEA flight to Paris, then change to the Air France flight to Lima as it routed via Pointe a Pitre the capital city of Guadeloupe, a French colony in the Caribbean. Here, Chris would leave the plane and I would continue to Lima. Chris's family owed a sugarcane plantation on St. Kitts and his uncle owned the local airline that hopped around the Caribbean islands like an air taxi, so he thought he could hop on one of these to get home to St. Kitts.

As we journeyed home for Christmas, we both had note books in which we wrote about the best places to hide on the train, plans for avoiding railway officials and how to get from Paddington Station to Heathrow Airport; taking loads of film on rolls with our Kodak camera. We knew we needed to save our pocket money to pay for a taxi for this segment of the journey, as the Heathrow tube link was yet to be built.

Well, that was the plan, a pair of 11 – nearly 12-year-olds with clarity and ingenuity, and very vivid imaginations!!

Heathrow airport was the tricky element, getting through customs and onto the plane without being spotted!! By 1966 Air France had Boeing 707 jet aircraft on the route, with Trident jets used by BEA (British European Airways, or as some called it Britain's Excuse for an Airline!!) (BEA later merged with BOAC to become British Airways as we know it now).

Although there were twenty or so boys and girls on the train (Cheltenham Ladies College was the girls school), Chris and I decided to wander up and down the carriages, finding hiding places and working out how the doors operated on the toilets. The Guards van would be impossible to hide in as there were always men on duty sorting out the post bags. Our only option was to hide in the toilets, and move around the train to avoid the guard and ticket collector.

When the train pulled into Paddington Station at twelve (I wondered if the station was called after the bear from Peru?) we were grouped on the platform by the teachers who were supervising. Half an hour later another train pulled in. It came from Southampton, and I saw Harriet get off giggling with several other very pretty girls. She looked different somehow. Well she was three years older than me so was now fourteen and she had grown up.

'Hi Charlie,' she said and introduced me to her

friends. 'This is my famous wayward brother, master escapologist and causing mayhem at school,' the girls all tittered and giggled as they all said, 'Hi Charlie.'

I introduced Chris to Harriet as he would be flying with us as far as Point a Pitre. Harriet, I found out later, had made Chris and I heroes, as we had the gall to escape from school, so all her girlfriends saw us as adventurous.

A porter arrived behind her with her suitcase and another bag, as she said goodbye to her friends.

'Come on scroate, let's find out where we get a coach to Heathrow. We have to check in by two.'

My teacher met Harriet and gave her my airline tickets and my two passports to look after. Yes, we had to have two passports; one British and one Peruvian. We would leave the UK on our British passports and enter Peru on our Peruvian ones, and if the planes went through Chile, then we were to use the British passports there as well, as Peru and Chile in those days were not good neighbours.

We were travelling as unaccompanied minors, and as such we both had to wear this enormous plastic tag on a long lanyard around our necks. I thought it was cool, but Harriet didn't like it and hid hers under her blouse. She thought of herself as an adult.

We found the coach station that would take us the final journey to Heathrow and then we needed to check in at the BEA desks for the short hop to Paris. We would be in Paris for a few hours before our Air France plane would take us home on a flight that would take over 20 hours. There was one stop en route and this was Guadeloupe where Chris would get off.

Harriet had several of her girlfriends from school going back as well, but she was told to look after Chris and I, and didn't want us to undermine her with her friends. She was annoyed at having responsibility for us. We got to Heathrow which then consisted of two large buildings, one called the Europa Building (to become Terminal 2 later) where we were catching the flight to Paris, and the Oceanic Building (later to be Terminal 3) for long distance International flights, and the airport had three runways in a triangle surrounding these two buildings.

As our flight was called at four and we boarded the plane our excitement grew. This was going to be a fantastic experience. My only other time in an aeroplane was the twin-engine Douglas DC3 'Dakotas' that Faucett Airways in Peru flew up the coast and into the mountains to Cuzco. For an eleven-year-old to be flying in a plane that had three jet engines was magical. We took our seats with Chris in the window seat, with me in the middle, and Harriet on the aisle end.

The flight to Paris took about an hour, eventually leaving at four thirty; it was so exhilarating to hear the whine of the jet engines spooling up as we lined up on the runway. The pilot released the breaks and we screamed down the runway, bumping and juddering as we went down, which seemed to take forever then suddenly it climbed at a very steep angle into the air. The view out of the tiny round window was fantastic and we saw how big London really was. Soon though we entered cloud and that was it for five minutes, as we continued to climb at a steep angle ... suddenly breaking out into brilliant sunshine over the tops of the clouds.

In no time at all the flight was over as the Captain announced that we were starting our descent into Orly airport. We landed an hour later and were met by Air France stewardesses who were all very tall and elegant in their light blue uniforms and stylish little hats. I knew that Harriet dreamed of becoming an air hostess when she left school so she was asking them lots of questions about the job and how she could apply. We were both tri-lingual and spoke French and Spanish naturally, as well as English.

We were escorted to a transit lounge and told we had to wait there for three hours. Our Boeing 707 jet was parked on its stand at the departure gate so Chris and I stood looking at it and observing what the ground crew were doing; how the bags were loaded and how the steps to the front and rear doors were accessed. Chris took yet more rolls of film on his trusty Kodak camera. We wrote everything into a ruled book too. An announcement was made in French at around eight fifteen that the Air France flight to Lima via Point a Pitre was ready to board, and the pretty air hostess came up to us and said that we were to board first. We all collected out satchels, bags and coats and followed her down the stairs, through the bottom doors and a short walk across the apron to the rear steps of the big airliner. We climbed up the stairs and waiting for us at the top was another pretty air hostess, who showed us to our seats. Chris said that I could sit next to the window this time and Harriet sat with her girlfriends the row behind us. There were about ten of us children in total as unaccompanied minors. We were all very excited too. This plane was HUGE, and we saw that the toilets were just at the back near to where we were sat. The galley was here too where the air hostesses prepared all the food and drinks.

This tall very tanned man with a huge handlebar moustache walked down the central aisle. He was dressed in a white short sleeved shirt and had lots of gold bars on his shoulders. The air hostess gathered our attention. 'This is Capitan Foucard, and he wants to welcome you all on board personally.'

The Captain was a handsome man, well the girls thought so! And his English was very good, tinged with a French accent.

'Welcome on board our Boeing 707. For those of you who have not flown with us before, we hope you enjoy your flight, and those who have, welcome back. I am hoping to be able to invite you up to the flight deck once we are in the cruise. But this is a night flight so the view out will be dark. And those of you who want to, can come up two at a time. Our flight time to Point a Pitre will be fourteen hours and I understand that two of you are leaving us here,' Chris put his hand up, 'yes it's me and Maize,' he volunteered.

'So,' the Captain continued 'we will be arriving

in Pointe a Pitre just about sunrise at seven and will be there for about two hours then we leave for Lima, which we estimate will be another six-hour flight. We will be in Lima for two pm. This Boeing 707 is a new one and so we have the newer jet engines. I want to ask you all to behave yourselves and my air hostesses are here to look after you during the flight.   Hopefully most of you will sleep too. Any questions or problems please ask them.' He stood up and turned to the air hostess, 'Genevieve a vous d'acors,' he said in French to her.   He saluted us and walked back to the flight deck saying hello to the other passengers as he went through the curtains that separated First Class from Economy.

There were eight air hostesses on board and to Chris and me they were all very beautiful. We had three that were specially trained to look after children, and as they settled us in and made sure our seat belts were secure and we had our tables locked into the seat in front, they came around with bottles of water for us.

All the passengers were aboard and they closed the two main doors. The chief air hostess spoke to us all on the loud speaker and welcomed us on board. She gave a safety briefing that we didn't listen too as Chris and I were too busy looking out of the window.

The aircraft suddenly started to move backwards as the tugs pushed us out of the parking place, and then we heard the four Pratt & Whitney engines spooling up.

We taxied around Orly Airport to the main runway, and the big plane lined up. Then with a roar all four engines came to life and we accelerated down the runway, until the captain finally pulled the aircraft into a steep climb and we were airborne.

After a while, sitting in the hard seats with all the other passengers, and not being able to see a lot out of the window, became boring. The highlight of the flight was when the Air Hostess took Chris and I to the flight deck. As we walked up through the cabin, we went into the First-Class area and saw how much bigger and more comfortable the seats were, plus everyone who was sat up here all looked very posh. She opened the door to the flight deck and stood to one side as Chris and I entered. WOW!!! What struck us first was how small the cockpit was and how many instruments there were all lit up. It had four seats – two were occupied by the Captain and First Officer, then there was the Flight Engineer and the Flight Navigator, both sat behind the pilots. The First Officer got out of his seat and he and the Flight Engineer went to get a drink and chat up the air hostesses. I took the First Officer's seat and Chris sat behind me looking between the seats. The Captain showed us the array of flight instruments and all the switches and it looked really complicated. He also showed us his maps and the route we were taking. We were at thirty-two thousand feet up in the air and the view forward was amazing. Although it was eleven o'clock at night the horizon could be clearly seen and the roundness of the earth at this height was brilliant. That was the very time I decided I wanted to be a pilot!

We spent about a half hour in the cockpit and the time went so quickly as the next group of girls were due in. We said our goodbyes and I asked the Captain if I could come back on the leg to Lima. He said to wait and see.

The food on board the plane was nice, well I thought it was, but Harriet didn't like most of it so she would pass her tray over to me when I had finished mine and we swapped trays, I would share her food with Chris. There was some food she liked, mainly anything fishy, which I wasn't that fond off.

We passed the time on the long flight by playing card games, I spy (which got boring quickly as there wasn't a lot to guess) and we read our magazines we brought with us like The Beano, before we got very tired and fell asleep. The air hostesses brought out blankets and covered us with them.

At five am, the Captain announced that we would be landing at Guadeloupe in an hour and that the descent would be a little bit turbulent due to the hot air even though it was early morning. We were served breakfast, which came out quickly and we were rushed to finish it. The plane started its descent and our ears popped, and it shook quite violently as it went through lower level clouds and levelled off. As the sun was starting to rise we could see the many different little islands in the sea. It was very picturesque. We seemed to fly around in a circle and finally made the approach to land at Pointe a Pitre with a very steep final descent as the airport is surrounded by mountainous terrain. We didn't realise at the time, but it was one of the hardest airports to land at and in 1962 an Air France 707 had a fatal crash here killing most the passengers and crew. We landed safely!! When they opened the doors, this wave of heat and humidity hit us like a hairdryer going off in your face. It was intense, and as soon as we disembarked the plane, we were drenched in sweat instantly. The terminal building was slightly cooler but not that much. We were herded together and told not to wonder off as we were only here for a couple of hours.

Just as we were saying goodbye to Chris, who was catching a flight in his uncle's plane to St Kitts, a man in a very colourful Hawaiian shirt, khaki shorts and a baseball cap on his head back to front walked up to us with a huge grin on his face. He was a short plump man with a deep tan, a big bushy beard and gold chains around his neck; lots of rings on his fingers, chewing on a big fat cigar. He looked like a gangster out of a movie. When Chris saw his uncle, he ran and jumped into his arms, and he was swung around several times in a big bear hug speaking to each other in French. Clearly, they had a very close bond together.

Chris came back to me and introduced his uncle. 'We need to photograph the terminal and write this up in the book. Can you do that on the Lima leg?' he asked.

'Sure Chris. Have a great Christmas,' and we embraced before he went off to find his uncle's plane.

Pointe a Pitre was not a huge airport and therefore Harriet, her school friends and I were sat in the departure lounge waiting for the plane to be refuelled and serviced before we could board again. Everyone around us wore very colourful outfits and some of the clothing was very lightweight cheesecloth and not a lot of it … well on the women. We looked very funny in our school uniforms, sat there hot, sweaty and bored.

The funny thing was that we took off from Paris at nine o'clock at night and we had flown for fourteen hours, but it was only six thirty in the morning here. We were given some chilled water to drink whilst we waited, and a new cabin crew and flight deck crew joined the plane here. Our outbound crew would stay here for three days before retuning on the flight back.

We were collected by yet more attractive air hostesses and taken back on board. The plane had been cleaned and tidied up, but we took our original seats with Harriet sitting next to me. The new Captain came up to see us, and introduced himself too, and he asked who Charlie was. I put my hand up, and he said that Capitan Foucard had left a note that I wanted to see the cockpit in daylight so he would be inviting me up once they were in the cruise. WOW!! A very excited 11-year-old!!

We took off from Pointe a Pitre and the big jet banked tightly round to miss the mountains and climbed to its cruising height. The cabin took a while to cool down with the air conditioning. Just after brunch, the air hostess came back to find me and Harriet who came with me to the cockpit. Again, I sat in the co-pilot's seat with Harriet in the Engineer's seat behind. The Captain was impressed at my knowledge of all the instruments and what they did, and the view was fantastic, as we were approaching the northern jungle area of Colombia with the Andes in the distance. He went through what I needed to study at school to get the right qualifications to become a pilot and said that I am already half way there with my knowledge. At that age, this was the encouragement I needed to really knuckle down and study hard.

But, later on I found out that a) my maths was poor and b) my Dad was dead against me becoming a pilot as he wanted me to become an engineer like himself. Well at 45 years of age I finally qualified for my Pilot's Licence, so got there in the end, bought a Piper Warrior single engine plane, and set up a flying school to boot!

We landed in Lima at around two thirty in the afternoon, at the new Jorge Chavez International Airport near Callao on the coast and there were Mum and Dad waiting for us. Mum broke down crying as I did too, and Dad hugged us both.

Our Christmas that year was exceptional, there were lots of house and beach parties planned with all our friends that we had not seen in nearly two years. We spent most of the holidays either at Villa Country Club on the coast or at the Lima Cricket Club, and ate BBQ food. We swam, surfed, skied, land sailed and rode horses bare back on the beach. I was back home in my comfort zone and all thoughts of Drummond College and the bully boys and deputies temporarily forgotten.

In early December, Dad had to go on business up to Iquitos – which was the capital of the Amazon jungle in the northern part of Peru, and suggested we all went with him, so that Harriet and I could experience the jungle region. We flew up in a Faucett Airlines Douglas DC3 Dakota. It was a frightening flight experience that took six hours in an ex-US Air Force plane with hard basket seats, green painted bare interior and few frills, although the air hostess did bring drinks and sandwiches for us. The twin piston prop aircraft was slow and as we climbed up through fifteen thousand feet to clear the lowest mountain peaks, a little green tube was pulled out of the overhead racking and we had to suck oxygen into our mouths for about twenty minutes as the plane droned over the Andes Mountains. The rest of the flight was over dense jungle until we landed at Iquitos Airport, all grateful we had made it safely. We were to spend three days in Iquitos and we booked into the only hotel in town, that was built on stilts. In fact, every house there was built on stilts as the Amazon River often flooded and it stopped the big creatures, crocodiles, snakes, and others from entering the houses. The temperature was high above 100f (41c) but it was the humidity that got us all. If we thought that Guadeloupe was high this was like walking through custard. We took a canoe ride up river, with Mum and Harriet and some local Indians who told us not to trail our hands in the water, in case they were eaten by the piranha fish that were in abundance in this part of the river; whilst Dad was looking at his engines that gave power and pumps to irrigate the fields and for fresh water. We saw the piranha fish eat a dog that had wondered into the river to drink water and was consumed in minutes; we saw huge crocodiles (or were they alligators or caymens) in the river and basking on the banks, and a huge boa constrictor snake. In town, there were loads of colourful birds and parrots, but the mosquitos and other airborne insects were a right pain in the neck. I loved it, but Mum and Harriet were glad when we boarded the plane back home.

Christmas Day was spent on the beach and we ate everything off the BBQ. No turkey or Christmas pudding though and no custard either … and certainly no Brussels sprouts, cabbage or swede, as they didn't exist in Peru in those days.

My 12th birthday was celebrated up in the mountains at the Granja Azul where they were celebrating the Dias de los Reyes Magos – or Epiphany to us Brits. Officially it is on the 6th January but they carry it over to the 7th to maximize customer visits. On this day, they had a traditionally cooked meal called a 'Pachamanca' where a huge hole is dug into the earth about six feet deep, it is lined with stone and heated with intense fire and charcoal; then food is laid in metal trays covered in moist banana leaves. This is all then covered in earth and a red rose placed on top and the food is then baked for ten hours in the ground. Then there is a great celebration with music and dancing and drinks until the food is ready. The chefs then dig out the earth and remove the food, which is placed on serving tables from which everyone helps themselves, using your hands to eat the food from wooden bowls. The food is delicious and the right words to describe the taste are not sufficient to paint you a picture. We ate lamb, chicken, pork, beef, Guinea pig – all marinated in special spices; plus, corn husks, not the sweet corn we know but much larger husks and a very pale yellow colour, sweet potatoes, corn bread, rice and baked bananas in their skins (called tamales) and other Andean produce, such as green lima beans or "habas", cassava or yuca, and humitas (sweet treat). We drank chicha which is a fermented drink made from maize, or for children they had chicha morada, which was un-fermented purple maize mixed with grape juice.

All the adults got very merry and we had to stay the night there. That was a birthday to remember as all our friends came up to the restaurant in the mountains. We played in their extended adventure park, rode on horses and fed the llamas and alpacas, and swam in the outdoor pool whilst our parents talked and danced and drank, getting very merry.

Two months whisked by in no time at all, and soon at the end of January we were back at Jorge Chavez Airport saying our sad farewells to our parents, with loads or regret and trepidation at having to return to the life which I now began to see as a punishment or incarceration. Mum was in tears and didn't want me to go back, Harriet couldn't wait to get back to her other friends, although she spent loads of time over the holidays with the school friends that were flying back with us too.

This time we flew back on a new service by BOAC on a Vickers VC10 via Miami to London, so I didn't meet Chris Wrigley on the flight back.

As agreed though I made loads of notes in 'The Book' and Dad had bought me a Praktica camera for my birthday with rolls of film, so I took plenty of pictures on the flight back.

We left Harriet at Heathrow as she was going back to school by car with some of her friends and I was escorted with a couple of other boys who were at other schools back to Paddington Station where we caught the train back to Cheltenham with a female 'minder' to look after me.

Arriving back at Drummond College was a huge anti-climax, and we found we had been moved into a new dormitory in the other house. Also, the Headmaster asked to see me on the second day back at school and asked if I would like to become a prefect, to look after the new first years. But I didn't as I wanted to stay with the 'Gang of Five', so I declined, which gave me a de-merit in the behavioural book.

CHAPTER FIVE
PLANNING THE NEXT ADVENTURE

Chris and I were pardoned for our indiscretion at placing the school under the embarrassing position of having had runaways, and our tuck shop and horse riding privileges were reinstated. We settled back into school life again, and the first few months were spent catching up with the gang of five, with all our adventures back home. We also met our new dormitory prefect. Apparently, Ames did not return from his Christmas break due to finances and stayed with his mother and new stepfather in Spain. We got a letter from him, thanking me for teaching him Spanish and telling us he was settling into a new school in Barcelona.

Angus McDonald was a ginger hair Scot who was 14 and introduced to us as our new dorm prefect. We were all now twelve, well I was just twelve as I had my birthday in Lima at a beach party. Angus seemed at first to be very dour, and he had a thick scot accent that we all struggled to understand. But we soon found out he was one of us, having been bullied for his ginger hair and his Scottish accent by the plummy mouthed snobs.

Surprisingly enough his nickname was 'Ginger' and that was what his family called him too!

As we were now a little older, we had become interested in the female line after having caught the Head Boy 'in- flagrante'. Titus and Tobias had smuggled into the school, hidden in the lining of their suitcases, some American magazines that would have been confiscated had we been caught with them. Shall we say they were not part of our educational reading material. They gave us an insight into a different world and we saw, for the first time, female under ware, nudity and other things too. It was lights out under the covers reading, and Ginger said that some of the pictures shown he had seen at his family's castle in Scotland with some of the female staff and his older brothers.

One very early morning Chris, Titus and I got up and sneaked upstairs to where some of the teachers slept, and we saw the bathroom door slightly open ajar, as it was not shut properly. We looked in through the crack of the door and saw Mademoiselle Fabien, in just her frilly French underwear, pulling up her stockings as she got dressed. It was thrilling and exciting and stirred parts of our anatomy that we didn't understand at the time!! She never knew we spied on her from time to time after that.

It was all harmless naughty schoolboy antics, that would merit the cane from the Headmaster had we been caught!

From an educational point of view, I suppose I was improving. My vowels and pronunciation were becoming very public schoolboy with a slightly plummy accent, and my Spanish accent was slowly disappearing. I had my pet subjects; French (due to the very attractive teacher and visions of her without clothes on); geography, because it was very interesting; history was OK; English was a necessity. Religious Instruction was fascinating, as I was born in a staunch Catholic country to Protestant parents, who founded the Church of the Good Shepherd in Lima amidst the fury of the local religious zealots in Lima. The subjects I hated were maths, Mr. Rowlands scared me with his chalk missiles every time I lost concentration, which was often; Latin and Greek – pointless learning dead languages; and Physics and Chemistry, the only fun side was experimenting at blowing things up in the labs.

Head Boy introduced a couple of new deputies,

and one of them singled me out as a potential target, undoubtedly instructed to do so by the Head Boy, the other new deputy picked on Chris and Titus; interestingly neither attempted anything when Kando was around as his stare alone frightened them.

One evening, Chris and I were completing our homework in the study, when two of the deputies barged in, holding their small canes in their hands and tapping them on their legs as they walked around us. We sat still at our desks and waited to see what they would do. Deputies were there to keep good order and ensure that we were doing what we were supposed to be doing, and therefore had a right to ask to see work or inside our desks.

As the deputy walked around the back of me he pushed me in the back on purpose. I didn't react but just sat there pretending to work. He stood over me from behind and picked up my work book and dropped it on the floor.

'Whoops,' he said as Chris and I watched him. I didn't pick it up.

'Pick that book up Latin boy,' He said.

I didn't react.

'If you don't pick that book up you are in detention for a week.'

I turned to face him in my chair and stood up. My height placed me slightly taller than him, and he raised his cane to hit me. I grabbed the cane from him and broke it over my knee. His face wet ruby red, and he stammered out:

'You are for the high jump now Dashwood. Breaking a deputy's cane is an offence that the Headmaster will need to deal with.'

I leaned into his face and just three inches from his nose, I said quite calmly 'OK – we go now to see Mr. Langhorne and you explain why you went to hit me, and Wrigley is my witness,' Then looked at the other deputy and added 'I suppose you will come too, won't you and back up your friend here, so it's our word against yours.'

I picked up my school work and satchel and put my school coat on and went to go, but the deputy hesitated.

'We will leave it for now Dashwood, but know this …. your cards are marked.'

'You will have to stand in line behind the Head Boy and all the other deputies first,' I jeered, and sat down again to resume my studies, knowing that what we had on the Head Boy would protect us. This episode created a need to go to war against the deputies.

Very early one morning Chris and I sneaked out of the dorm and down to the kitchen. There hanging up from hooks in the roof were these rolls of fly trap, which were about two-foot-long and coated with horrible sticky stuff that flies flew into and got stuck on. We climbed up on stools and removed two of them, we also found some rotting cabbage and swede in the bins from yesterday's meals and put some in a bag.

We sneaked back up to our rooms and once everyone had made their beds we hung back from going down for breakfast until all the boys had left and we found the beds of the deputies who had threatened us yesterday in study, and put the fly traps in one bed and the rotting cabbage and swede in the other. It would be a nice surprise for them tonight, having had a full day to fester.

That evening there was a huge commotion on the landing outside our dormitory and a lot of shouting. The Head Boy was called as was Matron and our lights came on as our door smashed open.

'Who has done this revolting thing,' said Matron to all of us. We all pretended to be so innocent and

104

sleepy we just shook our heads and went back to sleep. They never did find out, but those deputies never troubled us again.

Chris and I also spent some private time in the study late at night or after lights out pulling our information and pictures together into a coordinated sequence which allowed us to start planning our next escape. We had to be very discreet so that no one caught us otherwise months of plotting and planning would have gone out of the window.

We started by placing the photographs in an album in the right order so that we could follow a plan based on what we had seen visually. We tabled all the major stumbling blocks in our way that would cause catastrophic failure of our plan, and we highlighted the section from Paddington to Heathrow as one, and security at Heathrow and getting onto the plane as the biggest challenge, if not the impossible or even implausible part of the whole plan. Once we were on the aircraft and it had taken off there would be no going back in our eyes as we could persuade the captain to take us to at least Pointe a Pitre. We learnt huge lessons on the aborted now famous Hot Air Balloon Roundabout escape. The main one was not to trust any adults as they often lie. This through the eyes of 12-year-olds!

Our planning was meticulous and we discussed long into the nights how we were going to execute the next attempt. We decided to go by rail to London, bus to Heathrow then chance our luck to bypass all the security checks to slip through the ground base operations to board the jet when everyone's attention was on cleaning and preparing the plane for the next flight, and we would hide in the rear toilets. We found through our observations on all the flights we had taken over the Christmas break that the crew changed over leaving the aircraft empty for about 20 minutes. This would be the window we would have to get on board and hide in the toilets. We hoped that they would think the toilet lock was jammed.

So, over the next three weeks we would walk to Lansdown Station and observe the station staff and guards and the trains to see when the optimum time was to jump onto the train before it left. Again, we would start the journey at the end of the train near the guard's van and work our way forward during the journey from one toilet to another, hopefully being unseen.

Titus, Tobias and Kando were getting very suspicious of our nightly secret meetings and they approached us one day after games. They thought we were getting too close and up to no good, and did not want to believe that we were homosexual.

Chris and I burst out laughing, so much so, we were in stitches. We then swore them to secrecy and told them of our plan to escape again. They all said that we were 'The Gang of Five' and we should stick together, but then if Chris and I did want to try again – they would support us and hide our escape for as long as possible to allow us to get away.

We set the date for the attempt in three weeks-time, just as the new May Bank Holiday exeats were allowed and most of the school would see the boys go for long weekends to friends and relatives. We five had nowhere to go so we would be staying at school with a skeleton staff on duty to supervise. Aunt Joan had gone to Italy on one of her religious jaunts.

School life was still very hard, and during those early spring months we were finally getting used to the politics and the culture of being at boarding school with fifty other boys. As a 'gang of five' we did protect each other and the deputies and prefects chose to leave us well alone now and instead picked on the new and vulnerable weedy boys. We sometimes felt sorry for them and on occasions we warned the prefects or deputies to lay off a certain boy, on very rare occasions using our hold on the Head Boy to stop any bullying. But we didn't allow anyone to penetrate our bond of five.

We were all now twelve and in the last two years our bodies had begun to fill out. Kando was now nearly six-foot-tall and just as broad; he had immense strength and competed in weightlifting. He was the star number three in the scrum in rugby, the school relied on his speed and agility on the field as well as his bulk and strength to obliterate the opposing teams I was number eight in the scrum and Titus and Tobias were fly half's and wingers. In hockey we were unbeatable, and were gradually building a reputation in the inter-school's games that we were super humans. The five of us together with Ginger made up 6 of the eleven players, and we were ruthless on the pitch. Were we dirty players? … others thought so … we didn't … we were adventurous, clever and more skilful with our hockey sticks than the competitors were, so much so the umpires could not keep an eye out on all of us! Kando was an immense barrier in all his goalie's outfits, Titus and Tobias were forwards, whilst Chris and I were on the wings, left and right. We seemed to have a telepathy between us and we skilfully flicked the ball to each other, instead of just bashing it as hard as we could. The school PE teachers and Headmaster thought we were champions and all the school bullies hated us for it. We used it to our advantage.

Around the school, as we were together in the same classes as well as dorm buddies, we did stick together, almost never being in a position where we were on our own. Kando was just pure brawn, huge hands and scary with his jet-black skin and African looks; Titus, short and very thin, always had his hockey stick with him; Tobias average height but rotund, not fat, but a bigger bone structure, was taught how to use a rope on his Father's ranch in Texas, and Chris, tall and skinny like me, carried a piece of bamboo, that was highly polished and he could weald this swiftly so no one saw it coming. I didn't have any skills, so just used my height as I was nearly as tall as Kando and my dark Latin looks. NO ... please don't get us wrong ... we were not vigilantes nor were we out looking for trouble, but in the environment, we lived in at school, meant we had to protect each other; otherwise we would have been severely beaten, caned or abused by the older boys.

It did not stop us from playing some pranks though. One of these was to fill balloons with water and hang out of our dorm window, or from the fire escape platform, and drop these balloons on senior boys or prefects as they walked underneath, quickly hiding after we had released them.

We also went into the other dormitories and made "apple pie beds" where you turn up the bottom sheet half way so that when you try to get into the bed, your feet either go through the sheet or you can't get into bed properly. It was a scream to hear the boys complaining. We never got caught.

One of the other boys in the dorm across the hall had placed socks in the teacher's toilet upstairs, and blocked it, which meant that they had to use ours. We used to wait by the door to watch Mademoiselle Fabien come down in her French frilly nightie to use the toilet and our eyes followed her back up the stairs when she had finished.

Lessons were varied. Geography was always

interesting as the teacher kept us fascinated by his adventures during school holidays when he went off exploring new countries and filled our heads with wild imaginations. He also invited us to talk about our home countries so that everyone shared our experiences. French was our favourite, especially for Titus and me as we were fluent and Mademoiselle Fabien favoured us. We both had schoolboy crushes on her and often had some wet dreams about her too, spying on her at night.

Maths was the worst subject, as Mr. Rowlands was scary and brutal, he made the subject difficult to understand, but we had the measure of him by now and every time he threw a piece of chalk or the blackboard rubber at us, we would stand and scream at the top of our voices, so that teachers from other classes would come running in to see what the commotion was about. This only made him worse though!

The other subjects we got along with, but at the end of this year we had our first exams to take.

We tried to keep out of trouble, and off the Head Boy's radar, but inevitably we did cross swords with the deputies and prefects from time to time.

The May weekend approached and Chris and I started to prepare for our next adventure. We agreed that the gang would fill our beds with clothes and towels to emulate us sleeping and Ginger was told to stay asleep so he could not be incriminated in the eventual investigations.

Chris and I got ready for bed as usual, changing from our uniforms into our jeans and sweat shirts with our pyjamas over the tops. We cleaned our teeth then packed everything into our small rucksacks bought from Gamages the month before. Titus and Tobias had 'acquired' several Marathon and Mars bars, and some cans of Coke. Tobias even raided the kitchens and got some chicken drumsticks and ham in a container for us as well. Lights out at nine-thirty – so we all got into our beds and pretended to be asleep when matron did her rounds and switched off the hallway and bedroom lights. We waited until ten and Kando got up and did a quiet recognisance to make sure the coast was clear.

He came back with his thumbs up, and the gang whispered their 'good lucks' and 'goodbyes', as Chris and I stripped out of our PJ's and put our duffle coats on. Tobias opened the sash window to the fire escape and we climbed out silently onto the metal landing and down the stairs. We paused at the bottom to listen for any movements. There was someone in the kitchens, and we looked through the bottom windows to see the Head Boy and the kitchen maid back in business.

Chris signalled we should go, so we headed for the Amphitheatre at the end of the playing fields and stopped to make sure we were not followed. We then slowly made our way around the streets bordering the playing fields on the main road that led us to Lansdown Railway Station. We arrived at the station side gate used by guard's and staff and found it still open. The nine forty London train was waiting at the platform. Chris and I knelt behind a trolley piled with boxes and waited until the guard started to walk towards the front of the train leaving the guard's van clear. We jumped out of our hiding place and into the guard's van, then into the first toilet cubicle on the right-hand side of the corridor of the last carriage. As this was the last train tonight for London it had 12 carriages all with individual compartments off a long corridor and at either end was a toilet behind a small door. Each carriage was connected to the next with a walk through travelling platform over the couplings. We heard a whistle blow and another, then the train lurched forward and slowly pulled out of the platform. We were on our way.

We both looked out of the small window in the

toilets to watch when the train was clear of the station. We heard the guard talking to someone, then the sliding noise the compartment door made when sliding it open. 'Tickets please.' he said in a monotone voice.

We listened at the door until he had cleared all the compartment along this corridor. We needed to get to the next toilets at the end of the next carriage without being seen. We peered out of the door and saw him disappear through to the next carriage and noticed he didn't check the toilet doors as he went through. This would be a good sign. Before we went through I told Chris to hang back a bit as I went into the guard's van and found on a little desk an 'OUT OF ORDER' sign, so I pinched it. I returned to Chris and said, 'Look what I've found,' and showed him the sign. This would come in handy later.

We went quietly down the corridor of the carriage and slipped into next toilet on the corner of each carriage end. We locked the door and Chris sat on the loo as I stood and listened at the door. We stayed there for quite some time, before we heard the conductor say over the speakers that they were approaching Cirencester Station. We used the Out of Order sign whilst the train was in the station. It held for quite a long time and we started to panic a bit, as we heard people speaking quite loudly.

But eventually the train slowly pulled out of the station and we could breathe again. We decided to move up to the next carriage after the conductor had gone. We waited until he had passed our toilet hiding place, and then moved up the carriage. We found an empty compartment and opened the sliding door and sat near the window looking out at the dark countryside. We did see a couple of people walk past and look at us sat there. Can you imagine what they were thinking; two twelve-year-olds on their own, late at night on a train in jeans and duffle coats with duffel bags to match!!

'Hey Chris, I don't like the way those people looked at us, let's go into the next toilets and travel to London that way.   The next stop is Swindon, so we need to use the Out of Order sign again.'

'Yes, good thinking. If they report us to the conductor or guard, we will be caught.'

We slipped out of the compartment and through the next carriage and into the far end toilet. We were now in the middle of the train. The train chugged slowly along the tracks, and it seemed to take forever to get to Swindon. We eventually heard the announcement that "we were approaching Swindon and any passenger leaving the train here should take all their baggage with them."

We opened the door and slipped the sign onto the door handle. The train came to an abrupt halt, and we heard steam coming out from the carriage. We waited to hold our breaths.

There was a great commotion outside, we couldn't see anything as the toilet window was very small, but we heard a lot of heavy boots walking through the carriages. Someone said: 'The two young lads were sat in the next compartment down, officer.'

'Right you lot, I want every carriage searched, and all the toilets too, anywhere these two lads could be hiding.'

Chris and I looked at each other, very despondent.

'Looks like the game is up Chris,' I said. 'Do you think we should give ourselves up?'

'Seems like the best thing to do. But we need to learn from this. It's the furthest we have got so far.'

We came out of the toilets. And stood in the corridor waiting for the guard to approach us. It was a policeman that came up to us. 'Are you Dashwood and Wrigley?' he asked. We nodded our heads.

'You had better come with us then. You are in lots of trouble back at school you know,' he said with a smile on his face. 'Come along now, we have to drive you back to school to see the Headmaster.'

Then another policeman shouted, 'We have found them. 'Come along you lot – we can't delay the train any longer. Off you get and back to your duties.'

We were escorted off the train and as we stood on the platform the train guard, an older man in his dark blue uniform and cap with a grey moustache who looked like he was an Army Officer, came up to us and said, 'Well that's the first time in my 20 years working for the railway that we have had two runaways from school, and you managed to out-smart me too, you clever boys.' He had a huge grin on his face and ruffled our hair with his huge hands. He wasn't angry at all.

Chris then volunteered the sign to the train guard.

'Excuse me sir, but you had better have this back I suppose. Sorry if we caused you any delays.'

I said, 'yes, I am sorry too, but all we wanted to do was to get home to see our parents.'

The guard and policeman both bent down to our

level and asked, 'where do your parents live? London?'

'No,' said Chris, 'mine live in St. Kitts in the Caribbean and Charlie is the boy from Peru, his parents live in Lima.'

'So how were you going to get to Peru and St. Kitts' the policeman asked?

'Well you see, we had it all planned. We get off at Paddington, get a bus to Heathrow and catch the BEA flight to Paris, then Air France to Point a Pitre and it goes on to Lima .... simple as that,' I answered in a very grown up matter of fact voice.

They both laughed out loud at this, as did the crowd that had gathered around us and had heard my statement.

'Well, I have never heard anything like that before,' said the policeman 'How did you get airline tickets for the flights home?' He was curious.

'We don't need any,' said Chris 'we simply walk on the planes and hide in the toilets until they take off then they have to take us home as they can't turn back.'

More laughter, everyone was now talking at once and they all started asking us questions:

"Where are your parents now?"; "does your school know?"; "which school are you from?" "how long have you been planning this for," etc. etc.

The policeman stood up and said to the crowd.

'OK, Ok, Ok, that's quite enough now. It's very late and we have to get these two young rascals back to their school.'

The crowd disappeared and the nice guard jumped into his guard's' van, blew his whistle and as the train slowly pulled out of the platform, he gave us a huge wink and a salute and shouted, 'good luck lads ... you will need it.'

The policeman took us through the station entrance to the front of the station where there was a dark blue Rover waiting. There were around seven other police cars also parked or about to leave as well, showing the size of the police presence on the train.

'Get in the back you two,' he said and we slid into the back seats of the big Rover. The policeman got into the front passenger seat and said to the driver, 'come on then George, let's make our way back to Cheltenham.'

'Can we have the blue light on?' asked Chris.

'OK but not the siren as it's too late and you are not technically an emergency,' George the driver said.

The policeman who found us turned around to speak to us.

'You have caused quite a commotion you know. Once your school matron realised that you had escaped, the Headmaster and Head Boy had to beat your friends into telling them where you had gone. It was pure guesswork that we found you. Someone reported that they saw you at Lansdowne Station and we had to rush to Cirencester to meet the train but just missed it, so we called Swindon for back up to hold the train there and we arrived as the train was pulling in. George here is going to start a new career as a racing driver soon,' he laughed.

'Did our friends rat on us then,' Chris asked?

'No, they did not. Apparently, it was one of the deputies who had been spying on you working on the plan that found it under your mattress. Your pals all kept shtum. That's loyalty for you.' he said.

'Well you both have a very keen imagination thinking you could get all that way home. Are you both that unhappy at school?' he asked.

'Yes and no,' I answered, and Chris added, 'it's an adventure to see if we could pull it off. We tried two years ago and got picked up at the Hot Air Balloon roundabout, so we have spent nearly two years planning this.'

'Oh, right …. that was you two? I remember hearing about that. A lorry driver caught you.'

'Yes, that's right,' Chris said.

'What will happen to you when you return to school then,' he asked?

I replied very matter of fact, 'a telling off by Mr. Langhorne followed by twelve of the best with his cane, and removal of all privileges for the rest of term. So, no tuck shop, no riding and a dormitory guard at night.'

'Wow, that sounds like a prison,' he said astonished.

'Well that's right − it's called a borstal, or boarding school. No difference,' Chris replied.

The policeman was silent for a while, then he said.

'Mm … The Boy from Peru … that will go into my report. I like that. Bit like Paddington bear escapes,' he laughed at his own joke.

We drove quite fast all the way back to school, and when we pulled up in front of the school door it was gone three o'clock in the morning. The Headmaster and Matron were standing there with very serious faces on. We got out and stood next to each other holding our duffle bags by our sides.

121

'Hello Headmaster, here they are, safe and sound
…. The little rascals. I have to say that what they have
done is wrong, but they deserve a medal for ingenuity.'

'Yes, yes officer. That may be so, but they don't
need encouragement,' he was clearly very angry.

Matron said, 'now both of you go and have a
bath and then straight to bed and don't wake the other
boys up.'

Mr. Langhorne grabbed my ear, twisted it and
lent down to put his face into mine and said, 'I will see
you in the morning, both of you, in my office at eight
o'clock,' and he shoved us inside.

The policeman said as he got into his car, 'good
luck lads,' and waved as he drove off.

We went upstairs to the communal bathroom on
the first floor, my ear was burning from where the Head
had grabbed it, so it hurt like mad. We got undressed and
into a hot bath that was ready for us. We washed and
changed into our PJ's that Matron had left out for us,
then we tiptoed into our dorm to get into our beds.
'Welcome back,' said Kando, then they all started to
whisper loudly.

'AGGHAMM …' came from the doorway.
Matron stood there. 'No chatter now boys, just get some

sleep, especially you two Dashwood and Wrigley, as you are for the high jump tomorrow. Good morning,' and she closed the door.

We promised to tell all in the morning and we were so exhausted that we fell instantly asleep.

BANG, the door to our dorm flew open and banged on the wall. Stood there was the Head Boy whipping cane in hand, tapping it on the side of his leg.

'The Head wants you two in his office now. No need to get dressed, just put your dressing gowns on,' he said in a menacing voice.

We got out of bed still very sleepy, but with the thought of the inevitable caning we would both receive after a gruelling talking to about the school, its reputation, the disgrace on ourselves and our parents and all the other guilt trips he could think off. We didn't really care, as what we did last night was dead exciting and we both wanted to try again sometime.

We were led into the Head's study and stood to attention in front of his desk. In his office stood his secretary (his wife), Matron and the Head Boy. He was writing something with his ink pen. He stopped, used blotting paper over the ink to dry it, and handed two letters to his secretary to send off.

He looked up at us, pointing to the letters in his secretary's hand.

'Those are letters I have regrettably had to write to your parents, informing them of your dreadful deeds and that anymore of this and you will leave me with little options but to expel you both. DO YOU UNDERSTAND ME,' He shouted these last words at us? He then stood up slowly and started his speech that we were expecting, but then surprised us.

'I am not going to lecture you now. I have called a full assembly of the whole school at nine this morning where you will be publicly punished. I want you to go and get dressed into your best school uniform and stay with Worrall. Now go.'

An hour later we were in the main school hall where we had the main assembly. All the teachers were there on the stage, and all the boys were in their class groups each with a prefect. Everyone was excited, and the noise level was very high, expecting that we were going to be publicly punished. This was a very rare occurrence.

The deputies were stood at the front of the boys on the main floor. Chris and I were held on the side stage by Worrall, as the Head marched on stage. The noise level in the hall suddenly went silent and you could hear a pin drop.

The Head stood in the middle of the stage and addressed the boys, his hands in front of him, with his long black Headmaster's gown on and his funny cap too…. in full regalia as someone said.

'It is with great sadness that I have been forced to call this full assembly. Never in the hundred-year history of this well respected and exclusive college, have we had to endure the disgrace and damage to our reputation by two of our own. Not only do they bring dishonour to their families, but they dishonour every single one of you boys standing here in assembly.' He paused and looked around at the teachers behind him 'And to all the excellent and devoted teaching staff too. And as Headmaster of Drummond College I will not be able to hold my head high at the next Headmasters conference in London. Dashwood and Wrigley have brought this shame on us. And this is not the first time they have attempted an escapade from school either. It leaves me with little alternative than to try and dissuade them from attempting this again. Their punishment will be twelve strikes of the cane in front of the whole school. They will also lose their privileges at the tuck shop and will be locked in their dormitory at night along with their accomplices. Now come here boys and take your punishment.'

He stood aside as Worrall brought us onto centre stage. We agreed we would not cry and we were prepared for the cane.

'Wrigley, you first,' the head said.

Chris stood in front of the whole assembly and looked up at the gallery and not at the boys. Worrall told him to bend over and grab his ankles as the head removed his shorts but left him in his underpants. He stood back and aimed the cane at his bottom.

THWACK, THWACK … twelve strokes of the cane. Chris stood up afterwards on the very edge of tears, his face bright red and his bottom clearly hurting. He was told to stand to one side. He hobbled across to the side of the stage.

'Dashwood, your turn now,' said the Headmaster.

Worrall stood in front of me, and whispered 'You deserve this Dashwood … teach you to spy on me,' and with that he pulled my shorts and my underpants down, and the whole school sucked in their breaths so loudly, you could hear it. Before I bent over, I stuck a piece of hard rubber in my mouth and grabbed my ankles. I felt the tip of the cane tickling my bare cheeks. I braced myself for the first blow.

THWACK it came and I stood up involuntarily as the shear stinging pain bolted through my body.

'OW,' I said and the whole hall giggled.

I turned to look at the Headmaster as if to say that didn't hurt and deliberately slowly bent over again.

THWACK ... THWACK ... THWACK came the second, third and fourth in quick succession. I stood up again, looked at the Headmaster, and defiantly pulled my underpants back up. I looked back at the Head Boy then back to the Headmaster without commenting. This clearly angered him even more. I resumed the position and before I could brace myself again they came in quick succession ... Ten more!! I had fifteen strikes of the cane, five extra for insubordination. But on the last stroke the cane snapped in two. And the whole school gasped as did half the teachers. I stood up with tears welling up in my eyes and spat the rubber out at the Head Boy.

I was so close to bursting out crying, but held it all in.

I pulled up my shorts and could barely walk back to the side of the stage as the Head said something to the assembled boys. The pain was unbearable and I had never felt anything like this before. We were taken by Matron to the school medical centre to have the whelps cleaned and treated with iodine and a soft padding attached to both cheeks. We were unable to sit down on chairs for four days, and had to stand in all our classes and to eat.

Some of the senior boys and prefects thought it was highly amusing, but the first years were terrified.

Due to the caning, we were unable to swim, and I missed a big swimming competition between our three rival schools and we lost. I also could not run properly for several weeks afterwards so couldn't play summer hockey.

Two weeks after the caning I received a letter from my Father. He said he was very disappointed in me and that I had let him and my mother down. The Headmaster had also charged him with the cost of a broken cane! In the letter, Father said that coming home was not an option and that I needed to knuckle down and concentrate on my studies so I passed the 'O' Level and 'A' Level exams for University. He added that if this happened again, the Headmaster said that we would be expelled, and this was not something he would condone (whatever that meant). Mum also added on the bottom of the letter that she was annoyed with me and that I was to behave, but she missed me.

Next letter was from Harriet, which was very short and to the point. She said that I was not clever attempting to escape and how stupid could I be if I thought we could have sneaked on board a jet plane home.

Well that told me!!

Chris had similar letters as well.

CHAPTER SIX
A YEAR OF PEACE

Over the next few months Chris and I agreed to keep our heads down and let the dust settle after our second failed attempt to escape. But the urge to do it again was so strong.

We had to go over our plans again and look at where we slipped up and how we can succeed next time.

Chris and I found out a couple of days after our return that the gang had hidden all our books and photographs behind the radiators. The Headmaster and form teachers spent a week questioning Titus, Tobias, Kando, Ginger – then Chris and I about how we executed and planned the escape. But we gave them very little. We said that we just went out the window.

Ginger was replaced by a deputy head boy on our dorm, and the dorm was locked at night for the next three months, with the deputy having a key if one of us needed the toilets. Also, the whole school were watching us, and we had a huge following by the rank and file boys who gave us big respect.

We understand from some of the better senior boys that although we were not named as such, the

130

papers got hold of the story of two runaway boys and made up a story about it. The Headmaster was not pleased at all as it named our school. After half term, our privileges were returned to us and we could buy sweets off our allowance from the tuck shop and we got back into horse-riding as well.

But we were watched all the time by the Head Boy and his deputies.

June through to September in 1966 was a very warm summer and after our welts had healed from the caning, we got back into school life, enjoying games and studying hard at most subjects.

We had the summer break at the end of June until the end of August, and I spent half the time with my Aunt Joan in the Forest of Dean, and then I got an invite from Titus to stay with his Aunt and Uncle in a town called Saumur in the Loire Valley. Chris, Tobias and Kando all went home for the summer holidays. My parents could not afford to fly Harriet and I home, so she spent the summer months with some rich friends in Nice and went to Monte Carlo as well.

Aunt Joan was a very large lady, a spinster, very knowledgeable and kind, but she really did not know what to do with me. We went to visit castles and ruins in the Wye Valley and we explored the countryside visiting pubs and galas in nearby villages. She made her own wine and beer and liked a drop every now and again … well every night. We played games in the evenings, cards, Waddington Go, battleships and cruisers, and Cluedo. She also had a television in black and white and we watched the news. Life at her cottage was lonely as she spent some of the time working on her lessons for next term at London University, so I used to go down the road to see farmer Jones and help him milk the cows. I remember one day, I was bored, so she said in her shrilled voice, 'Charles, I will pay you a penny for every dandelion head you pick out of the grass.' Armed with a bucket and a trowel, I went around all the lawns surrounding her house and cut out all the dandelions. I then noticed that there were many more in the field next door, so I picked those as well. And the grass verge from the little green at the top of the hill had loads, so they were placed in my bucket too, and the house down the road where an elderly lady lived on her own was totally cleared of any dandelions. Several hours later, well most of the day really, I returned to the house and spread out several old newspapers over the kitchen table, and started to count each one out of the bucket and onto the table. I had a piece of paper and pen and noted every 20 dandelions counted so I could keep track. In the end, I had over five hundred dandelion heads and proudly told Aunt Joan who was clearly bewildered. 'But Charles, I only wanted the dandelions cleared from my own garden, not the whole of Monmouthshire!' she exclaimed. 'But you didn't say that,' I replied, 'you just said all the dandelion heads I could find.' Still she paid me £5.00 which was a lot of money in those days and my very first wage. I later learnt from Father that Aunt Joan had charged him for the money!

Aunt Joan was so relieved when we got the letter from Titus's Uncle and she asked me if I wanted to go. 'YES please', I said too eagerly. She telephoned to accept and made the travel arrangements. We drove up to London in her little Morris Minor and stayed at her little cottage in Essex. The next morning, we drove down to Gatwick Airport and she put me on a BUA (British United Airways) flight from Gatwick to Le Touquet. It was a new service using the small BAC 1-11 jets and took about twenty minutes. When we landed, Titus was there with his uncle to collect me. It was wonderful to see him.

It took us nearly six hours to drive to Saumur in his uncle's Citroen, pass Rouen, through the winding roads of the Normandy countryside, stopping off for lunch at Alencon and again briefly at Le Mans where the famous motor-race is held, reaching their village of Parnay on the south bank of the Loire to the east of Saumur just after five in the afternoon. It was a long car journey, but Titus and his uncle told me stories of the family and what they did in Parnay, and when we got there I fell in love – twice!! Once with the place itself and then with Titus's cousin Chantelle, who was a year older than me.

She was very French and very beautiful, slightly shorter than me with hazel green eyes, light brown shoulder length hair and a round face with such smooth slightly tanned skin. I was hypnotised by her. When we arrived, she came up to me and shook my hand and at the same time kissed me lightly on each cheek, blushing slightly. I learnt a lot from her including how to "French Kiss" with tongues.

The farm the la Croix family lived on was partly arable, although they did have cows for milk, some sheep and a couple of goats, that they made cheese from, plus the usual clutch of hens and geese, but the main crop they grew was grapes for the local wine cooperative in Saumur and the Ackerman Cellars.

Titus's uncle Pierre was a tough brawny man with a huge handlebar moustache and he was always very jovial, grinning and found everything very funny. He had a belly laugh at our stories of school. Madam la Croix, Louisa, was a tall elegant lady with beautiful porcelain skin and soft hands. It was obvious where Chantelle got her beauty from. She was a ballerina when she was younger, but now taught dance at the local girl's school where Chantelle and her younger sister Marie Clare went to school.

Titus and I shared bunk beds in the spare bedroom, and we had a very enjoyable five week on the farm. We helped with the plantations, the irrigation, we learnt how to drive the tractor and, as they also had stables and seven horses, we rode every day. The farm cottage was picturesque and old, having been in the same family for five generations. It had bougainvillea and ivy growing up the walls outside and the whole farmyard and garden areas were kept very tidy.

With Chantelle, Marie Clare, and an older brother Jean Paul who was fifteen, the five of us spent most our time riding down to the River Loire on the horses and fished, swam and raced around freely. It was just perfect.

In the evenings, we were given glasses of red or white wine mixed with water with our food, and at weekends, Tante Louisa would lay out a huge long table in the garden under the trees as Oncle Pierre would barbeque an array of food, chicken, rabbit, lamb and pork, with sausages and hamburgers. The neighbours would descend on us and there would be twenty or so people eating, drinking, dancing to a guitar and a violin that some people played. As the sun shone and the birds flew around ... simply heaven!! It was the best holiday EVER!!

One evening Chantelle wanted to check on the horses and asked me to go with her. Titus and the others giggled. We got to the stables and she did do a quick check on the stable doors, then took my hand and lead me into the small barn. There she stood on a small bale of hay and put her arms around my neck and pressed her lips against mine. Hers were so soft but I had never kissed a girl before. She said in French, 'first time hey?' then, 'OK I show you in broken English.' We embraced again, this time her tongue slipped into my mouth and I copied her. I was a VERY fast learner!!

After that we met regularly and kissed when no one was looking. My heart beat faster every time I saw her, and I suppose she was my first true love.

During the third week, Titus and Jean Paul had to go into Tours with his uncle to see the dentist, so Chantelle suggested we go for a ride. We saddled up the horses and cantered down the lanes to the river and round to where there was a small beach area. This was still on their land and was only reachable by horseback or tractor, so we had the area to ourselves. We tethered the horses near the long grass on the top of the bank and Chantelle suggested we skinny dip in the river, and before I could say anything she stripped off her blouse and jeans, and all her underwear and all I saw was her beautiful figure and petite bottom running into the water. She dived in and then surfaced and shouted at me to get a move on. I stripped off and ran into the water too and it was cold. She swam up to me and as I was taller my feet could touch the bottom so she put her arms and wound her legs around me and we kissed again. Even in that cold water, I felt something stir in my appendage and she just giggled when she felt it. At thirteen, nearly fourteen she was starting to develop into a beautiful lady and already had rounded but firm breasts, with very erect nipples. 'You can touch them if you want,' she said as I held her in my arms in that cold water. I really didn't know what to do or where to look, but it was my first introduction to the fairer sex.

We swam around then laid on the bank in the long grass, touching and kissing – that's all!!!!!

On our return to the farm, everyone was home, and that night Oncle Pierre announced that we were all going on an educational visit of the famous French chateaux in their region. The next day we all piled into the Citroen DS with three in the front and four in the back, so it was really squashed. We first went to see Azay-le-Rideau, a beautiful chateau surrounded by a lake; then on to Chenonceaux with its four arches spanning yet more water, partly in the river, and finally to Chinon where we also had some food and refreshments. That was a full day with lots of walking and it totally blew my mind at the beauty of the buildings. Whilst Pierre and Louisa walked slowly holding hands, we kids ran ahead and jumped on every wall, and looked in every room and dungeons of every chateau. It was a very fine day out and the sun shone for us and kept us very warm. In the car, we had all the windows open and it was so great when Chantelle held my hand discreetly in the car. Only Titus who was sat in the back with us noticed. When we got home that night, Oncle Pierre said that next week we would go to Blois (as he had business to do there) and go to the most impressive of French chateaux at Chambord, Cheverney and Chaumont.

We often went to Saumur town as well which had its own castle, but mainly for shopping in the fruit and veg markets.

One day, Oncle Pierre took Titus, Jean Paul and I to see a neighbouring farmer about half an hour's drive away, and when we arrived there was an old wooden hangar and a strip of short cut grass. Sat outside the hangar was an old Tiger Moth bi-plane and we were told that the farmer would take us up for a flight. As the chief guest, it was my turn first, so I put on an old leather helmet and goggles, and climbed into the front seat. The farmer jumped into the back seat, wiggled all the control surfaces, pressed a button and the engine leapt into life, with wind billowing in your face. He pointed the nose down the grass track and in seconds we were airborne. He climbed to a couple of hundred feet then banked steeply so we could wave at them on the ground then we went off and around the Chateau at Chambord before returning and diving steeply back into the grass strip. I jumped out elated and handed the helmet to Titus, then Jean-Paul had a go. It was a great surprise and totally exhilarating, and once again fuelled my ambition to fly.

Our time in the Loire Valley with the la Croix family was soon to come to an end and both Chantelle and I cried in each other's arm. My first true love. We promised to write to each other, which we did for six months, then she found a new boyfriend!!

Saying goodbye to Monsieur et Madame la Croix was very hard, and both Marie-Clare and Jean-Paul gave me big bear hugs too. They all invited me back with Titus for Christmas, but I knew that I was going home to Peru.

As Titus was returning with me, Oncle Pierre drove us to Tours Airport to catch the Air France Caravel flight back to Heathrow.

Our magical summer holiday was over and we came back to reality with a mighty big bump!

We were welcomed as usual back at school. In assembly, the Headmaster made a little speech about school work and the importance of hard work and studying, and hoped that there would be no more "adventurous exeats" as he put it staring at Chris and me.

The gang of five were kept together again in the same dorm, but we had a new prefect called Rupert de Long. He was half French and was pleased that Tutus and I spoke fluent French. He was OK and blended into our group very well.

We slowly got back into the routines and yes, I still removed the offending vegetables off my plate but this time onto Rupert's as he loved them all. This saved my rotting pockets and my odour as well.

Worrall was still Head Boy and his deputies but he took a different attitude towards us this term.

Two weeks into term, I was asked again by the Headmaster if I would tutor the first years in school practices, as he thought it might settle me down. I did as it didn't entail too much time and meant that I had to keep my eyes on them for the first two months whilst they settled in. This also meant protecting them from the third and fourth year bullies.

In the fourth-year boys, there were a couple of particular bullies who liked picking on the first years, and one afternoon we were in the pool for recreation, when these bullies came in and started to push the first years who were just sitting on the edge of the pool. Kando went up to the ring leader and suggested they stop picking on them, and was pushed back into the pool. We saw this happen and the five of us got out of the pool and approached the bullies. We surrounded them and forced them backwards into the pool, and then discovered that they couldn't swim. They never were bullies again, well whilst we were around at any rate.

The first years thought we were heroes.

Chris and I resumed our occasional night raids to the kitchens, and on two occasions we caught Worrall with the scullery maid again kissing in the kitchen. I made him aware that we knew and the deputy in our dorm was taken to task for sleeping through our adventure. We heard Worrall shouting at him in the study, asking how we managed to get the key to open the door and why he slept through the whole thing. The deputy was unaware that Kendo had slipped a sleeping pill in his night-time Ovaltine drink.

Worrall was very worried about our knowledge and we said nothing to him except just stared with a knowing grin on our faces so that he got the message.

Chris and I did review our grand plans once we found a new hiding place for them, and decided that it would be very foolish to attempt another go this year. We looked at weather charts and temperature charts and timetables and decided that May or June again next year would be the best months.

As October neared we were all looking forward to our next visit home for Christmas and the thought that we only had two months to go kept our sanity.

I wrote to Chantelle every week and sent her pictures of the school and told her what we got up to, and I got letters back from her as well. But they suddenly stopped in November and Titus had to tell me that she had met a French farm worker and was seeing him instead. It broke my heart.

Just before school broke up, there was scandal spreading around the school. Apparently, the kitchen maid was off sick, and we were told that she was pregnant and had named Worrall as the father. He was sent home early and we never saw him again. But this close to end of term, no appointment was made for a new Head Boy and the deputies had the opportunity to apply for the role, so were given different tests to do.

We had some success in swimming as we won the Champions Cup in the public school's tournament. As swimming Captain I was thanked and applauded in assembly in front of the whole school. We also did well at hockey too and for the third time this year I was on stage in front of the whole school with my fellow team mates. Mr. Langhorne presented me with the hockey cup for outstanding achievement, and as he handed it to me he said, 'well Dashwood, this is your rightful reward for a positive attitude. Please bear that in mind for next year.'

The Headmaster was still worried about Chris and I!!

As we were going to be elevated to third year students next year, we had new privileges bestowed on us. And at thirteen, we were allowed out on Sundays into Cheltenham.

This was to be a new experience for us all as we started to mature into young gentlemen. We would learn manners and deportment, how to greet people of higher rank, how to use cutlery, and how to behave in society.

CHAPTER SEVEN
HOME AGAIN

The end of November came and it was time for us
all to pack our suitcases and head for our homes around
the globe. We said our goodbyes to the teachers and
other boys, and the gang of five headed once again to
Lansdowne Road Railway Station to catch the train to
Paddington. Chris and Titus were flying via Paris on Air
France to Guadalupe, where Titus would catch a
connecting flight to Cayenne and Chris's uncle would
take him to St. Kitts; so, they went down to Gatwick
with Kendo, who was catching the BUA flight to Lagos.
Tobias and I went to Heathrow to catch our flights
home, he on TWA to Dallas, Texas and I on BOAC to
Lima. Harriet met me at the airport and came bustling in
with her loud friends. I hadn't seen her in almost a year,
and again she had changed. She had lost her girlie fat
and had become quite an attractive woman, with long
blond hair is a stylish cut, full breasts and a curvy figure.
I was quite proud that she was my older sister.

'Hi Charlie, you rascal,' she said taking me into
her arms and squeezing me tightly. 'Gosh you've
changed a bit,' she said looking at me. 'They been

145

sticking you in a bucket of manure or something, because you have grown much taller, and broadened out a bit. Quite the handsome brother,' I was delighted she noticed.

'And you have too Letty, gosh you are quite a proper woman now,' I said as a compliment. She ruffled my hair and took my hand to introduce me to her girlfriends, most of whom would be travelling with us to Lima.

Tobias just stood with his mouth open looking at Harriet, then gave out a wolf whistle, 'darn gone it Charlie, yawl have a mighty pretty sister, there,' he said in his Texas drawl.

'Letty, this is my friend and room-mate Tobias, he is from Texas. Toby this is my older sister Harriet,' I made the introductions.

Harriet introduced me and Tobias to all her friends who giggled a lot.

'Now, his is your famous brother, the escapologist is it Letty? We have heard all about your daring escapades Charlie,' one of the prettiest of Harriet's friend said as she touched my hand. 'You never told us you had quite a handsome brother Letty,' they said.

146

TWA called the flight to Dallas and Tobias said his farewells, adding, 'you lucky sod Charlie, flying home with a bevy of beauties,' and winked at me, raising his hand goodbye to the others.

We had to wait for an hour before our flight was finally called, and we were sat at the back of the VC10 again and all together with Harriet sat next to me.

The flight back was long, eighteen hours with a short stopover in Kingston, to refuel and take on passengers.

Mum and Dad were waiting for us at the airport when we landed. Dad had organised a special pass with one of the government officials he knew to give them access to airside so they were waiting just inside the arrivals hall before customs and immigration. We were escorted through the VIP lounge and Harriet and I felt like film stars. All her girlfriends were very envious.

Carlos was at the wheel of a new car, a Rambler, and by comparison to the police Rover or Oncle Pierre's Citroen, it was massive. Mum wanted to know all the news and about our flight, and the usual comments on how we had grown. Dad was quiet on the drive back to Gonzales Larrañaga. When we arrived home Maria and

147

Juana were there to greet us and gave us both huge hugs.

Our cases were taken to our rooms and Dad asked to see me in his office, so Mum and Juana took Harriet up to her room.

Dad was in a sombre mood. He had a lot of papers on his desk, one I saw was the letter from Mr. Langhorne and another on police headed paper, plus he had copies of the newspaper articles.

'Why Charles? Just answer me ... why? Are you that unhappy at school that you have to resort to this kind of behaviour?' Before I could answer he continued, 'The school is embarrassed and your mother and I are dreadfully hurt by your actions. You have brought disgrace on the school.' Picking up the newspaper articles, 'and you now have a police record for wasting their time, which heaven knows when this will come out. I am disappointed in you Charlie. This school is costing us a lot of money to give you the education I never had, and you are throwing it in my face. So, what have you got to say for yourself. Hey?'

He sat there quietly and I gathered myself together trying not to cry.

'I am sorry Papa, but the school is really awful. They make you be a servant, the food is disgusting and

148

all the senior boys have canes that they beat you with. The five of us are picked on and bullied because we are not from Forces or Diplomat families, and the Headmaster caned us naked in front of the whole school. I hate it there. Why can I not go to the school my other friends are at in England,' I was quite eloquent and spoke without a hint of a Spanish accent.

He sat looking at me. 'I am aware that the Headmaster used the cane on you, as we had to agree to some form of punishment, but not that he made you undress first.'

'No Papa, the Head Boy Worrall removed my shorts and underpants and the Headmaster started caning me five times before I stood up and pulled my underpants back up before he gave me another ten. I was very badly hurt and it still is sore.'

'Well, they never told me that. It is inhuman to cane you directly onto your skin. That's not right at all. And did Wrigley also receive fifteen strokes?'

'No Papa, he only gotten strokes. I got fifteen because I stood up to recover my underpants and he said that was insolence.'

'Mm mm … I shall write to him then if this is true.'

149

(In those days there was no internet, text messaging or mobile phones, just telex and telegrams or letters)

'OK Charles, we will not speak of this again, but promise me you won't try something like this again.'

'Yes Papa,' was all I said – so technically not lying, as it could have been taken as "yes, I will try this again, Papa"!!

Over the Christmas holidays I told my parents all about Titus and the summer holiday in the Loire Valley with his family, and all the chateaux we visited and showed them the pictures I had taken. Mum and Harriet picked a couple up and were looking at the pictures then to me, then back at the pictures.

'Who is this lovely young lady Charlie?'

I blushed a crimson red from my neck upwards.

'Oh, my god no Charlie,' said Harriett, her voice going up several octaves as she leaned forward and started to get very excited. 'Is this your first love Charlie. The way she is looking at you taking the photographs shouts out that she fancies you.'

'And look at this one Harriet. I think your brother has discovered love,' said Mum, as she found one that Titus had taken of the two of us kissing by the river with

the swing made from a piece of rope with a thick branch
tied at the end that dangled from a branch of the tree that
stretched out over the water.

'Oh, little brother, you've kept this a secret,' said
Harriet teasing.

'She is Titus's cousin and she is a good year
older than me, and she has a new boyfriend now
anyway,' I stammered back.

I had an open invitation to go back to Parnay
with Titus this summer, so I begged Mum and Dad to let
me go for the full two months and not go to Aunt Joan's.
Dad agreed as it was costing him too much with
"dandelion fees" as he put it. It was agreed and the
second letter Dad had to write was to Monsieur la Croix
to give his blessing and the Headmaster to inform him
that I would be going home with Titus in July.

Harriet also had a great time in Nice and Monte
Carlo, with her rich friends. The pictures she had were of
big boats, boys, restaurants, cocktail parties and loads of
girls in pretty summer dresses. He best friend was Lady
Cecilia somebody and her parents were stinking rich and
members of the aristocracy. Harriet behaved like them
sometimes. Still over the Christmas break I would not

see too much of her as she went off with her cronies into Lima society.

I hooked up with my old-school pals and we did the same as usual.

This year Dad had to go on a business trip to Lake Titicaca and asked me if I wanted to go with him on a boys bonding trip out, so he and I went to Juliaca and Puno, the girls didn't fancy it.

Dad and I took off from Lima on a Faucett DC4 and flew into Inca Manco Capac International Airport in Juliaca. The scenery as we flew over the Cordierras Mountains and the Andes to the lake was stunning and I spent the whole six-hour flight looking out of the window.

We were staying in Juliaca where Dad's customers were, but he had to drive to Puno as well. The only ferry on the lake was built in Britain and had Dad's engines on board, plus he had a major project on with the Peruvian Government for a hydroelectric plant nearby.

Lake Titicaca straddles the border between Peru and Bolivia in the Andes Mountains and it is one of

South America's largest lakes. It is the world's highest navigable body of water at twelve thousand five hundred feet high. The air is so thin up there that it can make you feel very dizzy so all the cars and lorries and train's carry oxygen balloons. It is also said to be the birthplace of the Incas and is home to numerous ruins. The lake's waters are very still and have a brightly reflective surface. Our guide said that surrounding the lake are national reserves sheltering rare aquatic wildlife such as giant frogs.

Whilst Dad was talking business, the wife of the owner took me to see the lake and we went for a ride on a reef boat on the lake. It was an incredible experience as the waters were so still it was like a millpond.

We were only there for a couple of days before flying home to Lima. On the flight back Dad asked if we wanted to spend Christmas at our favourite coastal resort called "Paracas," which was a good five hours drive south of Lima near Pisco, where the Peruvian alcoholic firewater was made. Paracas was a wonderful resort as it had everything there, pools, tennis courts, horse-riding, surfing and we had our own chalet as well. The food was always good too. When we got home Mum and Dad agreed that we would spend a week in "Paracas".

They gave Carlos, Maria and Juana Christmas off to go to see their families in Ayacucho in the Andes. Our house in Lima would be empty.

Harriet asked if her friend Suzi could come, only as Suzi's family had gone to Chile to see her older brother and she wanted to stay in Lima; they agreed, but I wasn't allowed to bring any of my friends as there was no room in the car! I thought about the trips we made in the old Citroen with seven of us, and our car in Lima was twice as big!!

Again my 13th Birthday was spent at the Country Club de Villa on the coast with all my friends and we had a great beach party.

The Christmas holiday went so quickly, it was time to fly back to the constraints of my prison camp, Drummond College, in dark, cold, miserable England. Before we boarded the plane, Dad took me to one side and reminded me of our agreement.

'Charlie, please behave this year; no more escapades or running away, and please knuckle down and study hard as you will have exams at the end of this year and I want you to do well. If you have behaved by

June, you can go to France with Titus, if not it will be to Aunt Joan's. OK??'

I hugged him and promised to behave.

When we returned to school, we spent the usual week catching up with the gang of five and all our Christmas adventures. Chris and I promised to speak soon about our plans and agreed to discuss these without anyone else knowing. When we did eventually meet, he had been collared by his Mum and Dad and been given a severe talking to as was I. We agreed to do nothing this year except to plan the next attempt in April the following year. Besides we would be fourteen by then and with hard work this year we could save up enough money to buy proper rail and bus tickets.

The one surprise was that Worrall had been expelled and in his place the Headmaster had elected Rupert de Long as the new Head Boy, much to our delight. A week into school term, I was told by a prefect that Mr. Langhorne wanted to see me in his study in an hour's time. What had I done wrong now? I searched my memory for any mistakes or rules that I had broken, but could not think of any. Also, I could not find Rupert

155

either. It was with a very heavy heart, and feeling very vulnerable (I had gone to my dorm and put on an extra pair of underpants!), I waited outside his study. At the appointed time, I timidly knocked on the door and heard

'Come in Dashwood.'

In his study was Rupert, Matron, Mr. Rowlands and Mademoiselle Rubens, all sat with smiles on their faces … well all except Mr. Rowlands who didn't know how to smile.

'Ah Dashwood. Come in, come in; please do sit down.'

'What have I done this time Headmaster?' I asked and everyone tittered.

'Nothing boy, absolutely nothing to worry about,' he paused and looked around the room, and all the teachers nodded.

'Now, as you know, we have had to let Worrall go and de Long here has stepped up to Head Boy. He has requested that you be made a deputy for his new team, and although you are a year too young, as we normally select deputies from fourth grade, on this occasion, and as you have made such sterling efforts last term to stay out of trouble and work hard, we are going to award you with a deputies' post. It has not gone unnoticed the swimming and hockey accolades you have brought to the school last year and hope that we can keep the cups again this year.' He looked at me through his glasses down his nose.

'Well …. What do you say Dashwood?'

I was dumb struck. I could not believe what I was hearing. My only thought was that Papa would be so proud of me, so I stammered.

'Thank you, Headmaster, and thank you Rupert, too. I would be delighted to become a deputy for you.'

And that was how I became the youngest deputy in the school's history. Two major achievements with the school!!

I took to my duties as a deputy, but I insisted with Rupert that I would not carry a whipping cane, nor would I discipline boys with corporal punishment, as I didn't believe in it.

He accepted this and kept me with the gang of five in the same dormitory, except that I became the dorm prefect as well. Over the rest of that year, I gained a lot of respect from the other boys, especially the first and second years; but I also attracted criticism from the other deputies and fourth years' boys for being well-liked and bucking the traditional system in my elevated position. My strategy did work as I had more control over the boys under my wing than any of the other deputies, and both Rupert, the Headmaster and all the other teachers could see this. It forged the start of a complete re-thinking on the role of deputies and corporate punishment at the school.

Cleverly it also made me behave too as I took my new responsibilities seriously. But ... it didn't stop Chris and I from planning the next adventure!!

One of the privileges bestowed on deputies was that we could go into Cheltenham in pairs or threes on Sundays, to have some freedom. I chose Chris and Titus to accompany me each Sunday and we walked into town. At a little café in town some of the girls from the Ladies College also frequented this café as they were allowed into town under similar allowances from their school. This is where we met Millie again, who was the horse-riding school teacher's daughter, and her two friends Grace and Veronique. They were a year older than us, but they didn't know that. Over the weeks and months that year we met them on a regular basis in town, and became good friends. Millie and I kissed on several occasions in the bus shelter when it was pouring with rain. She asked me how I knew how to kiss so well, and was she the first girl I had kissed. I told her the truth and said that I had a girlfriend in France last year but it was over now. Millie was dead impressed and asked me to teach her some more, which I was only too happy to oblige … being a gentleman, of course!!

Grace and Veronique got on well with Chris and Titus, and sometimes the three of us were allowed to walk into town on a Sunday to meet the girls and spend a couple of hours with them in the park or the café if it was wet. Titus and Veronique had a lot in common and spoke French to each other very quickly.

I received a letter from Mum and Dad in April, and Dad said he was so proud to have received a letter from Mr. Langhorne informing him that I had been made the youngest deputy in school history and how well I was progressing at school. He said that I had his permission to go to France with Titus for the whole summer months, if Titus's family agreed and invited me

In July and August, Titus and I went back to Parnay, and had an amazing summer with his family. I was disappointed that Chantelle had decided to go to Spain to study Spanish at a senior college in Madrid and then spend the summer with friends in Marbella. Every downside has an upside though, so I was happy that Titus's older sister, Sabine, who was fifteen had come over from French Guyana to go to school in Melun, just to the south of Paris on the edge of the forest of Fontainebleau. She was very, very pretty, but as she was Titus's sister I was very respectful and did not want to rile my good friend; but then she turned out to be the biggest tomboy I had ever come across. Anything we could do she was simply better at. She got on with everyone, and had a lovely way of just touching you when she spoke so it held your full attention. I was smitten again!!

Oncle Pierre took us to visit more chateaux in the region and we went to Angers and Tours as well. They had family and friends in the surrounding villages and that particular summer was very hot, so we did a lot of socialising. We did some tours of local vineyards to taste their products versus ours. The cooperative run by the Ackerman Caves held a major Wine Festival over three days, where they expected supermarket buyers

from all over France and other European countries to
visit to place orders to buy goods. Each farmer who
supplied food or wine to Ackerman were invited to have
a stall and run product tastings all day. We were all put
to work in making cheese, churning butter, collecting
eggs and loading the truck with all of the farms produce,
which we then took to the festival. Tutus, Sabine, Jean-
Paul and I were instructed to man our stall and talk to all
the customers about our produce and our wines; this was
to be my first introduction to selling and presenting, and
we did exceptionally well; in fact, so well that Jean-Paul
had to drive the truck home to get Tante Louisa and
Marie-Clare to load more product up for us to sell. Oncle
Pierre was very impressed with my ability to switch
from French to English and then Spanish, even the
Italians understood me. It was terrific fun and we
worked very well as a team, but more to the point it
made me realise that if I could not become a commercial
pilot, I would get into selling.

As the summer holiday progressed, we were
treated to lunch at Oncle Pierre's friends farm across the
valley and I remembered that last year he took us flying
in an old Tiger Moth bi-plane. We all piled into the old
Citroen and drove the 50 miles to the farm. When we

arrived, my eyes came out on stalks at what I saw straightaway.

'Wow … look at that,' I said pointing towards the hangar. There parked in the sun was a gleaming blue and white 4- seater Piper Cherokee light aircraft. His friend Monsieur Graveaux had also extended the grass runway and it was mowed like a bowling green. Before lunch, the farmer asked who wanted to go flying, and Titus told him that I wanted to be a pilot, so Titus and Sabine jumped in the back seats, and I took the front left hand seat. It turned out that Monsieur Graveaux had flown in the French Airforce as a fighter pilot when he was younger before he inherited the farm from his parents, and now he was also an instructor at a local flying school.

We went through the start-up routine and he explained everything to me. He turned the key and the engine roared into life.

'We have to taxi to the other end of the strip so that we can take off into the wind,' he explained, so he let me steer the plane with my feet on the rudder pedals. At the end of the strip we turned to face down the runway. He held the plane on the toe breaks, put two stages of flaps in and did the final checks of the engine and the controls to make sure they were working smoothly.

'Ok ... we go now ... you will fly ... when the speed hits this here,' he pointed at the airspeed indicator, 'you pull back but very gently on the control column .... Ok let's go,' and he released the brakes. I had one hand on the throttle and one on the control yoke and the little plane careered down the grass runway, 'eh voila .... pull back gently,' he said, and the plane climbed gracefully into the air with ease. We climbed to about six hundred feet and flew circles around the farm to see everyone waving at us and Monsieur Graveaux took control back to waggle the wings as we went over. Then he gave me back the controls and told me to climb to two thousand feet. We flew around for about an hour seeing the sights of the Loire Valley and I had a lesson in turning, climbing and descending. As we approached the farm on the return, we did an overhead circuit, before lining up with the runway on what he called the downwind leg and he talked me round the circuit until we were lined up with the runway ahead and instructed me to reduce the airspeed with the throttle until we gently touched the grass with the main wheels then let the nose down as well and we slowed up enough to stop at the hangar end right along the grass strip … he only took control once as I was coming in too fast.

'Tres bien … tres, tres bien Charlie. You will one day make a fine pilot.'

That made my day … the grin on my face was stuck there for several days afterwards.

After we landed, we had a delicious lunch outside on the family table and around fifteen of us all ate the food Madame Graveaux and Tante Louisa had prepared.

Lunch in this sleepy part of France took several hours and we all had lots of conversations on many different subjects including talking about my life in Lima.

Unbeknown to me Sabine was slowly getting a crush on me as she was very impressed with what her uncle told everyone about my piloting skills, and listening to my stories about Lima. Later, that afternoon, she and I sloped off for a walk into the vine fields. When we were far enough away from the family, she launched herself into my arms, and kissed me on the lips.

I was taken aback at first and then she giggled and wrestled me to the ground on a piece of long grass.

Sabine was a strong girl and knew a little bit of judo. I was overcome when she tripped me over with a judo move. She slid her arms around me and said, 'Titus tells me you kiss all the girls back in England. So, show me how you kiss?'

Well now … I don't want you to be getting the wrong impression of this 13-year-old boy!!!!

We all returned from summer holidays with loads of tales to tell. Everyone had a great summer break with a huge variation of experiences and activities. The only upsetting story was from Kando, who had a real tough time at home. His Dad, being quite a personality in Nigeria, was arrested by the local police on trumped up charges, but was released before Christmas. His family were all very worried as the political landscape in Lagos was unbalanced. His father's business was seized and frozen, the rebels who wanted to upset his success were all arrested, and the business re-opened. But his father had to spend all the holiday time working, so Kando saw little of him. Sadly, Kando didn't quite understand what it was all about, but he was very subdued when he came back to school.

The second half of the year was pretty much uneventful. Every Sunday we were allowed into town and we met up with Mollie and the girls. We had an open air 'Amphitheatre' at the far end of the playing fields, and Chris suggested to the girls that we meet there one night after lights out.

On the agreed night, we waited until after nine thirty and used the emergency stairs outside the main hall window to leave the house, and we stealthily made our way down to the theatre. The girls were already there as their bedtime was earlier than ours.

We each went to a different part of the semi-circular seating area and sat on the cold stone seats and started to 'make out'. Well … just kissing and fondling really … we didn't do anything; you know …. daring!! We spent the most thrilling hour and a half with the girls that night, knowing that if we were caught, it would certainly mean a public caning and even expulsion. And as a privileged 'deputy' I had even more to lose with my record! But it was so thrilling and we got a real adrenalin rush from doing this as it was so against school rules!!

Millie wanted to do more, but I was too embarrassed at the time as I was still a 'virgin' and didn't know if she was too. When we went horse-riding at the weekends she would pull me into an empty stable for a kiss and a grope when her mum and the other stable girls were not looking. She was very daring and I got the impression she would soon tire of me!!

One of the great dangers at a public school is the constant threat of exposure from some of the other boys – especially the bullies, who roamed the school at breaks, lunchtime and evenings after study period, looking for trouble or to cause trouble. As a deputy, one of my duties was to protect the first and second years, from these bullies. This is where Kendo and Tobias especially were helpful, as the bullies were very aware of the three of us and kept out of our way. They no longer threatened us if we were caught on our own, because they knew by now the brotherhood we five had.

School work progressed, and we knuckled down to study hard. All the teachers reported to the Headmaster that the famous 'gang of five' were all studious and behaving as we should be; well I overheard a conversation between Mr. Rowlands and the Headmaster when they were talking about us. Mr. Rowlands was even impressed with us … and that is saying something!!

Our occasional night excursions to the kitchen continued, with the addition of making peanut butter and raspberry jam sandwiches, from this new product that

Tobias brought from the States. Peanut butter was precisely that butter made from peanuts and it was yummy. It's not exactly new as it was invented by the Aztecs, and first produced in the USA in 1890, but the product was very expensive and only available in the high fashion stores in the UK, so no one really tried it. But, the combination of peanut butter and raspberry jam was as delicious as banana and Marmite!

Oh … and the kitchen maid who was caught with Worrall had a baby girl apparently!!

This Christmas, Mum and Dad wrote to say that they were coming back to the UK, as Dad had to attend an important conference for his company. Dad rented a house up in Lincoln for the two months, and we spent some of our time exploring the Lincolnshire Wolds. We also took a week's holiday up the coast to Northumberland, which was all very nice, but it was freezing cold, and Harriet complained all the time that she was missing out on some friend's party in London. I loved the wild ruggedness of the coast from Alnwick where we went to Howick Hall and Bamburgh Castle to Holy Island where monks lived in a castle called Lindisfarne, and up to Berwick-upon-Tweed.

CHAPTER EIGHT
ENCORE UNE FOITE

I returned from our Christmas holidays a wiser, braver fourteen-year-old, to take up my duties at school as a well-respected senior boy in our fourth year.

Chris had got all our old plans out and had been busily updating them as many aspects of the journey and methods of transport had changed greatly. Train journeys were quicker with the new diesel engines and the underground had opened as far as Hatton Cross. We had pooled around twenty pounds as well. There was a huge amount to do.

Tobias had overheard us talking about it and asked us what we were up to. He knew more than he let on, so Chris asked me if we could bring him in on the plans.

We spent a couple of days showing him what we had and he thought it was very good and extremely exciting. He wanted in on the next attempt, and made investigations into flights from Heathrow to Dallas. The flight times were similar, except for the fact that they went from a different terminal building than ours.

I was becoming a bit doubtful as to the plan to try another escape, as I was finally settling down to enjoy

169

school life. The food … I got used to, and by being very firm with Matron and cook, telling them how it affected me making me feel sick, I finally could skip the cabbage, Brussels and swede. The lessons were good, some very interesting … apart from maths, and I was enjoying being a deputy as well.

And of course … there was Mollie, too!!

So why would I disrupt all of this with what I believed would be another failed plan. My dilemma was how to tell Chris and Tobias, to let them down gently.

However, Tobias was a great strategist and saw a huge flaw in our plans

'Yawl got the god damn times wrong,' he said in his Yankee drawl. 'If we go at night, the train gets into London at midnight and we will be exposed all night. Why not go at five in the morning and catch the five forty mail train to London? That has a box carriage for bags and parcels, which would be better to ride in to London as the train guard or inspector never go in there during the journey. The only dangerous time would be if they opened the doors to add or take out bags or boxes at the two stations it stops at.'

It was a very valid point and we decided we would go at five am in September. We then had the spring and summer to finalise the plans and as we all had exciting plans again this summer, with Tobias not returning to Dallas and staying in Scotland with Ginger's family instead.

Chris was going to join Titus and I in France at his uncle's farm again, but one of us had to sleep on a camp bed in the tiny bunk bed room, which was OK.

Titus told me that his parents were making plans to return to France later in the year, as the family clothing business was better run from France than Guyana. All their main customers were in Paris, Rome or London now, as their American markets had declined. It meant that possibly Titus would be moved to a French finishing school before university.

This clouded the summer holiday as none of us wanted to break up the gang of five, but then here we were, Chris, Tobias and I planning our third attempt to escape which we all knew would lead to expulsion. Later, when we got back to school at the end of August, we found out that Kando's family were forced to leave Nigeria and had gone to Nairobi in West Africa, where Kando was now at school. He left us all a letter he had written from his new home with pictures of his house and school. We were all very saddened and would miss the protection he gave us and his very candid advice.

This news along with Titus's announcement made me change my mind about the escape attempt, as the gang seemed to be breaking up. I changed my attitude and concentrated on finalising the plans with Tobias and Chris. In France, we told Titus what we were planning and although he didn't want to come he said he would help by covering our tracks. It was a good job too as we had two new boys in our dormitory and Titus stopped them from raising the alarm until two hours after we had gone, which gave us a head start.

Tobias loved the French way of life and his Texan attitude was akin to the Mexican laidback, tomorrow is another day ideal, which blended in with the French country way of living. Nothing was rushed, there were no time constraints and we just took every day as it came.

Ackerman had their wine festival again and the three of us took charge of the family stall and outsold what we did the year before, much to Oncle Pierre and Tante Louisa's plaudits. After the three-day festival, we had a huge party in the garden and all the neighbours came to eat French-style BBQ food, with a Texan twist as Tobias insisted on overseeing the cooking. (*He is now a famous chef in Washington with a chain of high-class restaurants).*

The three of us spent yet another great summer in the Loire Valley and I spent just a week with Aunt Joan on my return together with Tobias, as Titus's grandmother had passed away and the family had gone to the funeral, so we cut our holiday early there.

Tobias found Aunt Joan very odd and didn't really get on with her. He didn't say a lot to me as he thought she was a relative, but his body language gave him away.

Back to school and our focus became the planned escape. We continued with our classes and the school system, but we also learned that there was a move afoot in parliament to cease corporal punishment, and the canes were taken off all the deputies and prefects at our school in 1968. It was not until 1986 that the government agreed to implement a law banning corporate punishment in schools, although some private schools continued to use this until 1998 when it finally became law. This meant that we would not escape the Headmasters cane if we were caught and sent back to school!

173

The day before 'D' day we carefully packed the rucksacks we had acquired from Gamages. In addition, we agreed to dress in jeans and T-shirts with hooded sweatshirts over the top so we looked like any other teenager in 1968. Our rucksacks we kept in our lockers and our clothes we laid out inside our beds so that we could change into them in the morning. Titus agreed to stand guard for us. As we were fourth year students we no longer had room prefects and our dormitory was in the other house on the second floor and held just six beds. There was a fire escape conveniently right outside our dorm window and Tobias had used some bacon fat to grease the runners two days ago, so it was silent.

None of us could sleep that night and Tobias had one of these new watches with an alarm on it which went off at four fifty. We got undressed and changed quickly. Titus told the two new boys that it would be in their best interests to stay asleep. He then slowly opened the window that slid up on its sash quietly. The three of us climbed out, Chris in the lead, Tobias and then me. We went down the fire escape, paused at the bottom to make sure the ground was clear and swiftly walked the hundred yards across the main drive to the road that went directly to the station. We walked together slowly as if we were on our way to work. At this hour of the morning it was very quiet and we were looking out for police patrol cars mainly.

We reached the station, and as planned the mail train was already at the platform. We walked round to the back of the station and climbed over the goods barrier and onto the rail tracks to slide open the goods carriage door from the rail side avoiding being seen from the platform. It was a good height off the ground but we managed to get inside and close the huge sliding door. No one saw us. We looked around for the best hiding places and found several large trunks and packing cases that we could form a wall behind which we could hide.

There were quite a lot of cases, boxes and wooden crates in the goods van, so we could build ourselves some great cover if anyone opened the door from the platform side.

We were just in time, as we hear a whistle blow and we sat down on the floor as the train pulled away from the platform. Chris and I were close by but Tobias was at the other end so we couldn't see him. Having no windows, we didn't know where we were, although there were small slits in the door-ways that you could just make out objects as they went by. As the goods van was at the end of the train attached to the mail carriage, all the passenger carriages were in front, therefore there was no access to our van from within the train. At least we were safe as far as the conductor and the guard were concerned. Our only worry was if the doors were opened to retrieve or add more cargo at each stop. This train was scheduled to stop at Swindon, Reading, then Paddington.

As we approached Swindon the train slowly came to a halt with steam hissing out of the brake pipes. There was a lot of commotion outside the carriages as the train was popular with early morning workers in London. We heard approaching voices – then the guard unlocked the lever and slid the door half way open.

'You can put your bicycle in hear sir if you wish.' and he helped a man put a bike inside and leaned it against one of our crates. It was simply luck that he didn't spot us cowering low behind the crates. The door slid shut again and we hear the lever being pushed into the locked down position.

A whistle blew, and the carriage clunked together as the engine took up the strain and the carriages started to roll gradually picking up speed. We settled down. Tobias came over to us and offered some gobstoppers he had in his jacket pocket. 'This here is mighty fun, yawl hear,' he said, 'next stop is Reading, is it?' he questioned.

'Yes, and it's more likely that they will unload some of the boxes there.'

Tobias thought about this for a minute. 'OK, let's stack all the boxes labelled for Reading by the door and hide behind those for London,' he said logically, always a clear thinker. He was like this on the hockey pitch, he could see moves in his head, which was why he was Hockey Captain.

We looked at all the labels and moved all those for Reading towards the door.

Eventually the train pulled into Reading Station, which was a major hub way. Again, there was a lot of noise coming from outside and we laid flat on the floor covering ourselves with some old sacking that was left in the van. The giant doors slid fully open and light beamed in together with a strange warmth as well. There was a lot of commotion as the guard started to issue instructions to porters to unload all the boxes with Reading labels on. One porter commented on how organised they were as all the boxes, crates and trunks for Reading were neatly stacked by the door. The guard looked in and around the van, took his cap off and scratched his head as he thought about how this had

177

happened.

'Must have been the lads in Cheltenham that done it. I will make a note to thank them next time I am there,' he said. 'Right you lot put all the London crates in here and let's be having you. Quick, quick, we haven't got all day.' and on came as many crates and boxes as had come off. The door slid shut again and we heard the now familiar levers locked down. Soon we were pulling out of the station.

So far, so good, so safe.

Chris whispered loudly, 'we are nearly there, Paddington is the next stop. How are we planning to get off?'

Tobias had already thought this through. 'As soon as the train stops we jump out of this other door and onto the rail track, but we need to be very careful that another train is not on the next track. We then need to make our way to the nearest platform, and the busier the better as we will blend into the crowd. At fourteen, we will be taken for eighteen or twenty-year-olds.' He was so confident in his abilities.

We all wondered if the alarm had been raised at school and if the Headmaster had called the police again.

'I bet old Langhorne will be doing his nut right

now,' said Chris, echoing what we were all thinking about.

'Yes, he will be so bloody angry with me especially. We need to be aware that Paddington might be awash with police officers looking for us,' I said. 'So, best if we split up and make our own way to Heathrow I think.'

Tobias thought it was a good idea. 'I will take the underground to Hatton Cross and a bus from there. Chris, you take the bus from the station if you can, and Charlie you should find a cab as you look the oldest of us all,' Tobias – back in command of all the ideas.

'OK that is a good idea, less of a chance to be spotted then. We meet up at Heathrow Terminal Three then, by the entrance to the check-in area as we agreed on the plan,' said Chris. We all nodded our agreement.

The train slowed to a snail's pace as it crawled along the tracks, frequently stopping for a few seconds before starting again with a jaunt as the carriages strained on their couplings. Eventually we hear the station tannoy stating that the eight thirty from Cheltenham was arriving at platform four.

Tobias said to Chris, 'platform four is good as it means that our side here will be facing the open tracks

179

on that side.' pointing over to his right, 'will be the platform side. Be careful when you open the door, just in case there isn't a train already on platform three.'

As the train stopped suddenly, Chris and Tobias unlatched the lever and pushed hard on the sliding door and it opened enough for us to jump out. Thankfully there were no trains on platform three. We grabbed our rucksack and jumped onto the sleepers and round to the side onto the opposite platform.

'Walk slowly guys, don't run and keep your eyes on the ground and not where you are going. Stay cool,' Tobias said.

We split up a bit to give each other space and walked slowly down platform three. There was a huge amount of blue uniforms, which were a mixture of police and railway staff, all in a hurry going nowhere, looking at every single child, we pulled our hoods up over our heads to cover our faces. We passed several officers, who seemed to be in a frantic panic. We must stay calm. When we got to the end of Platform Three Tobias peeled off and got onto the escalator at the internal tube entrance and disappeared. Chris walked through to join the queue at the bus stop that had London Airport as the last stop, and I walked over to a taxi rank and climbed into the back seat of a black cab asking to go to Heathrow Terminal Three.

'That will be ten shillings my lad. You will have to show us year dosh first mate.'

I slid a ten-shilling note through the payment window to him. He took it without looking at me and signalled to pull out. As we were turning out of the station a police officer was staring at me, and I made the mistake of looking at him. Then in the distance I hear a whistle blowing. But we were long gone by now. I wondered if Chris and Tobias had made it.

The policeman did recognise me and called his station to report my sighting. He presumed that the black cab was heading for the airport and suggested that maybe the other two were also around somewhere, but if that was where the school headmaster thought we would be, then we be apprehended there. No sign of any of the other two boys though.

The taxi driver looked occasionally at me in his rear-view mirror but said nothing. It took about an hour to get to the airport and as we pulled up in front of terminal two, I saw quite a lot of police presence, but maybe that was security for you? I thank the cabbie and made my way to the check-in area and waited hidden behind some advertising boards until I saw Chris and Tobias. It was about thirty minutes later that they appeared through the main entrance of the terminal, and I left my hiding place and walked over to greet them. Within seconds we were surrounded by blue uniforms and an officer came up to us.

'Well, well, well, young lads. You have led us a merry dance indeed. Got to congratulate you three on your ingenuity. But I am afraid we have to apprehend you and take you back to the school. But I must warn you now that your headmaster is spitting feathers,' He was a tall jovial man in his late fifties, and the man in charge of the hunt.

There were suddenly flash guns going off everywhere as reporters based at the airport heard the commotion and came over taking loads of pictures.

We were taken in a Ford Granada, with two officers in the front, one the driver, and the three of us sat in the back. A flash bulb went off in my face as a photographer got a picture of us in the car. On the way, back the nice police officer turned in his seat to speak to us.

182

'Now you are not under arrest, but I am afraid you are in a lot of trouble as you have broken several laws.' He counted them off his fingers, 'Unauthorized travel on the railway; breaking and entering the goods van; causing unnecessary waste of police time and resources; travelling under age without supervision, to name just a few,' But he was smiling at us. 'Which are the two of you who have done this before?'

'We are,' Chris and I said together.

'You have a taste for adventure then. My, my, and at fourteen as well. Got to hand it to you guys for getting as far as you did. So, tell me as I am intrigued, how were you planning on getting on the flights?'

We explained our plans to him and he burst out laughing, not at us but at the audacity of the plan.

'We should enrol you into the MI5 as advisors on security and how to breach an international airport,' he laughed again shaking his head, 'in all my career as a police officer I have never come across this before. I will take this into my retirement as one of the better jobs I did,' and he laughed again.

We arrived back at school at three in the afternoon, and waiting at the school entrance was Mr. Langhorne, looking very angry; Matron looking cross, and the Head Boy, with a grin on his face. As we got out of the police Granada, a huge cheer erupted from all the windows of the upper floor, as all the boys were hanging out of the windows cheering us and clapping. The Headmaster ran outside onto the drive and looked up at them shouting something but we couldn't hear him due to the level of the noise. Outside on the road were TV cameras set up and photographers with their flashbulbs going off.

The Headmaster said something to the Head Boy and Matron, and marched inside shaking with fury.

OHOH!!

Rupert, the Head Boy, told us to go and drop our rucksacks in our dorm and change into school uniform.

'I am afraid you are for the high jump this afternoon. Head has wired telegrams to your parents at nine this morning when we discovered you had gone, asking permission to cane you and suspend you all. But from a personal view, and I will deny this …. but good on you, what an adventure,' he said still smiling. We were escorted to our dorm to get changed and were told to be outside the head's office in an hour.

We three looked at each other and shook hands

'Well better add some blotting paper to your

184

underpants to dull the pain from the cane,' I suggested to Chris and Tobias.

'We sure as hell had some fun though, eh. No one stopped me at all on the underground and only a woman stared at me on the bus, but that was it until I saw you guys,' said Tobias.

'Mine was straight forward too. I was lucky enough to get a seat right at the front of the bus on the top deck, so no one took a blind bit of notice of me. They all must have thought I was a hoodlum of some sort,' Chris said

'Me too, the taxi driver asked for cash up front, but then a policeman saw me in the back of the cab as we drove off and think he alerted everyone. Pity I could not get hold of you all to warn you (*no mobile phones in those days!!),* so I kinda guess it's my fault we were caught. Had that policeman not seen me it would have been a totally different outcome, and maybe we would be in the air going home right now,' I admitted guilt.

'Hey Charlie, don't beat yourself up about it. We had a gas and we were caught. That's it,' Tobias said matter of fact.

Chris added, 'he's right Charlie, don't go blaming yourself – as it could have happened to any of us. Let's just brace ourselves for the Headmaster's lecture and punishment.'

We were ready to go, blotting paper in place.

We stood outside the Head's office for quite a while, he was on the phone and it sounded like a long-distance call as he was shouting down the phone to be heard.

Eventually the door opened and Rupert let us in saying 'stand in front of Mr. Langhorne's desk please,' he had to be seen to be supporting the school's stance on this.

The Headmaster sat at his desk, looking at Tobias first, then Chris, and finally his eyes rested on me. In a very controlled and even voice he started:

'Dashwood, I see you as the ringleader here. We found all your planning papers and most of it was written by you, and Wrigley here. Mortimer, I don't know how you became involved in this and going with these boys, but as its your first time, I am willing to believe that you were coerced into going.'

Tobias started to speak, but the Headmaster put his hands up and said, 'I have not asked for a response, so do me the grace to let me finish.' He was still for a moment.

186

'Mortimer, I have spoken to your parents and they have pleaded leniency and made a sizeable donation to the school funds. You will be put on detention and have your privileges cut for this term. You may go now, so leave us.'

Tobias was not going quietly.

'Sir, I just want to have the opportunity to put you right on one point.'

'Enough Mortimer, I don't want to hear you. You have been dismissed.'

'God, dam it Sir,' he shouted back 'you Brits really do my nut. I am going to have my say, whether you like it or not SIR .... I was not coerced into going, in fact I pleaded with Chris and Charlie to be allowed to go and indeed I also helped with the planning. Now yawl accept that or yawl don't.'

The head stared at Tobias with his mouth open.

'I have never had so much trouble from you foreigners in all my time of teaching and heading up this school. That's what comes from an undisciplined upbringing in your jungle countries,' He had finally lost it.

Matron stepped in 'sorry Headmaster but I think you should moderate your language, sir. These lads are

British, well except for Mortimer who is American,' she stuttered in embarrassment.

He turned his head slightly to look at her too, in the same contemptuous face he gave us. He returned his gaze to the three of us.

'You have proudly put this college on the social media map. We are going to be the laughing stock of British Public Schools and by tomorrow we will be international news. I may even have to reconsider my tenure here as Headmaster after all these years of devoted service. What have I ever done to you to deserve this. Eh, Eh, Eh?'

We just stood there waiting for him to reach for the stack of canes in the umbrella stand.

I cleared my throat. 'Sir, Mr. Langhorne, it has no reflection on you personally sir, but the public-school system itself. We feel like second class citizens in this school and have had the brunt of prefects and deputies, and until de Long here, Head Boys as well. We three don't want to be here, we wish to be at home, it's as simple as that. I was greatly honoured when you made me a deputy last year and proud to have served as well. But the appeal of adventure got the better of us, from the years of planning to the actual event. We are sorry if we have brought disgrace to the school and to you personally, Sir.'

We stood rock still as he gazed at me. Eventually he stood and said.

'I am not going to waste my energies in caning you three, but you Dashwood, and you Wrigley are going to be expelled. I am awaiting confirmation from your parents. Mortimer, you will be staying on – thanks to your fathers very generous bursary. Now go back to your dormitories and help Matron pack your trunks and say nothing to the press or any other boys.' Looking at Rupert he added to him, 'see to this de Long.'

And that was it .... we were expelled!!

That evening we were in the Head Boy's study having supper in isolation, when Mr. Langhorne and Rupert with two teachers and matron entered the room. We both stood up.

'I have now spoken to both your parents and have informed them of our decision to expel you. You are both to remain here until your guardian Miss Joan Evans can collect you both and you will stay with her until your parents arrive in the UK. But you will both be in detention and not allowed to speak to the rest of the school.'

When Headmaster had left, Rupert opened a bag and took out the main evening editions of the papers:

"Teens Escape School"

Three schoolboys from Drummond College – Cheltenham, escaped in the early hours of this morning and were apprehended by police at Heathrow Airport attempting to board an aircraft to go back to their homes. The boys, who must remain anonymous for legal reasons, were aged 14 and came from Peru, St. Kitts and Texas. This is apparently the third time in four years that two of them have attempted an escape, the boy from Peru and the boy from St. Kitts. They had been planning this for some time and their extraordinary adventure started when they snuck out of school via the fire escape and got into a goods van at Lansdowne Railway Station in Cheltenham, avoiding being seen until they arrived at Paddington. A police officer recognised one of the boys catching a taxi and the school pointed to Heathrow as their destination. It is estimated that they managed to elude up to 200 police officers who had been looking for them since their reported absence from school at 9am. It is understood that they now face punishment and potentially being expelled from one of the most prestigious public schools in the country.

There were distant pictures of us being caught at Heathrow and one of us in the back of the Granada, with me smiling at the camera, and a third arriving at school with Mr. Langhorne.

Rupert then switched on the TV (in black and white) and we were headline news at nine o'clock. Our names were kept out but our pictures were on national TV. Fame at fourteen!!

We spent a week in Theydon Bois with Aunt Joan waiting for our parents to arrive. Mum and Dad met Chris's parents on the Air France flight as they boarded in Pointe a Pitre and could sit together, so they had exhausted the why's and wherefores. Chris's parents were a lot more philosophical than mine were.

CHAPTER NINE
NEW HORIZONS

Our parents were booked into a hotel in London, and unbeknown to me, Dad had received a letter from Monsieur la Croix – Titus's Dad, asking to meet them in London too.

They were over from Guyana and had been told by Titus what had happened and had also seen the news. Mum and Dad were concerned that they wanted to complain about their son's association with me, but it was for an entirely different reason all together.

Aunt Joan took us to London to meet our parents and Dad was livid with me. He was so cross that he had to spend money they did not have to travel eight thousand miles back to the UK to sort out this mess that I had willingly and conscientiously made. What he did not tell me at that time was that his company had also asked to see him in London, as he was being promoted to run the whole company from the UK and they were looking at returning home in a years' time. That piece of news came out much later from Harriet.

192

Chris's parents took him straight home with them on the next flight and he was put to work on the sugar cane plantation to learn the ropes, and eventually took over the business from his father when he retired.

Mum and Dad were saved embarrassment when they met Titus's parents, who suggested that I perhaps would benefit from finishing schooling in France with Titus.

And so, the arrangements were made.

My education was to be completed in France, with a plan to spend a year at senior school with Titus. I was to travel to Paris on the BUA flight to Le Touquet from Gatwick and then catch the French railway service to Paris, Gard du Nord. Here I was met by Titus and his father, and we drove south to Melun.

Monsieur et Madam la Croix had returned to France after spending fifteen years in French Guyana, where they had built a successful fashion business, and as Paris had become the hub of the haute couture industry they felt they could expand further by being here. Melun was where they originally lived before emigrating.

Their apartment in the centre of town was large and occupied three floors of a five-storey building. The first floor was the spacious living room, which had several very comfy sofas and a roomy kitchen/diner. The second floor had two large bedrooms and a bathroom, this was the parents room and Sabine's room too, and on the top floor were two more bedrooms and a bathroom, where Titus and I shared one room, and his older brother had the other room, but he was hardly ever there as he had started at university in Rouen.

The Lycee St Jacques in Melun was the best school I ever attended. It was co-educational, which meant it was a mixed school with girls and boys!! The French education was different to English ones and in the end, it suited me better. In one year, here I learned more than the past four years at Drummond College. Was it because I was much older? Or was it because the teachers wanted to teach you!

A typical day started by Titus and I getting up at six and running down to the boulangerie, to buy fresh croissants and baguettes for breakfast. Back home Madame LC laid the table with ham, cheese, jams, pulses, fruit and yogurts and we simply helped ourselves. Black coffee and juices were what we drank. We walked to school meeting other friends on the way, with our satchels across our backs and no uniforms.

Classes were an hour each and we had plenty of free time to study in the parkland surrounding the school or in the study classes. Lunch was an open table of cold meats and cereals and fruit, which you ate wherever you wanted to. At lunch time, we tended to congregate in the school hall if it was wet outside or in the courtyard and playing field if it was dry, and we had actual conversations about everything. For the first few months I was a celebrity with the girls as they all knew about my escapology stunts. The boys kept teasing me about this being an open school so I could leave when I wanted to; but you know, no one was at all nasty, rude, arrogant or officious. They were all lovely, warm caring people who actually wanted you in the school. That went for the teachers and the Headmistress as well.

They really cared about taking time to explain lessons to you, facts or history and even listened to your point of view. We were encouraged to think for ourselves and come to conclusions in our own time. No chalk throwing, no fagging, no prefects or deputies.

Yes, they had a Head Boy and Head Girl but their roles were different and you were elected by your fellow students as the most popular in the school. You represented the school at official events in the town and at other official visits.

In games I was an equal in rugby and swimming, but they also played soccer, a game I had never found interesting. I joined the girl's hockey team to some rubbing from the boys, but found popularity with my skills with the stick and found myself helping the PE teacher to teach hockey moves. So much so that the girls started to win matches against other schools.

Some of the girls were very pretty too!

It was a real eye opener and I wrote to Harriet telling her how happy I was. She was now seventeen and about to start university, but she came to Paris for a long weekend with some of her rich friends. She came and spent a night with us in Melun staying in Jean-Claude's room. She loved the la Croix family and the next day she visited the Lycee as well and was warmly welcomed by the Headmistress in assembly that morning. Satisfied that her young brother was behaving himself, she returned to Paris in the afternoon, and later reported to Mum and Dad that I was doing exceptionally well.

I really loved France, and in the end stayed two years there.

CHAPTER TEN

AND …

Mum and Dad did return to the UK two years later, and moved to a small village just outside of Lincoln. But a year later they moved to North London.

I was sixteen when I returned to England, and spent a final year at a grammar school in Hertfordshire, gaining 'O' levels in French and Spanish (there's a surprise); English, geography and RE; but failed maths, physics and chemistry. I never took Latin or Greek.

After school Dad gave me the option to go to sixth form college or one of the lesser universities, but I had enough of schools by then.

I joined British Caledonian Airways in 1971 at the age of seventeen and worked hard so I never looked back.

In 1974, I was able to take my parents back to Peru on an airline concession ticket and we stayed for two weeks on vacation, and that was the last time I ever went back home.

Titus and I remained very good friends for years to come, and I often went to see his aunt and uncle in the Loire Valley.

197

Chris, Tobias and Kando fell off the face of the earth and sadly I never saw them again.

At the age of forty-five, I received an email from my old school, Drummond College, stating that they had received a message for me. I asked the school secretary how they found me, and she told me that it had taken some time, but they traced me through Linked-In, the commercial social media sight. She wouldn't tell me what it was about and all she would say is that it was rather unusual. She gave me an address and contact details of the person who had found a package in my name. Intrigued, I called and said I would visit them in two days' time. They lived in Hull.

The day came when I found the house they lived in, and knocked on their front door. I was shown into their sitting room and offered a drink. They were in their late sixties or early seventies and both sat excitedly, with grins on their faces and started to explain.

'We were just walking the dog along the beach at Spurn Point, one of our favourite places to walk Barney the dog, when we came across this lying in the sand on the water's edge.'

They handed me the very bottle that I had thrown

overboard thirty-five years ago from the Reina del Mar, before we reached the Panama Canal. The rubber cork had been removed so that the message could be read, but everything was replaced in the bottle again. I was just amazed that it had travelled all the way round the world through three oceans to find me here in the UK. I explained this to the elderly couple.

'But what I don't understand is how you knew it was me that this belonged to,' I said to the couple, bewildered.

The man answered.

'Well, you are The Boy from Peru. I was the police officer that picked you up from Swindon Railway Station and on the way back to Cheltenham, you told me all about your escape plans and this bottle that you threw overboard on your way to England.'

I pulled the cork out and took the piece of Dinky toy card out of the plastic bag.

The message read in English:

"To who finds this bottle. My name is Charlie Dashwood from Lima, Peru. I no want to go to Inglaterra, but have no option. Please know it is not of my will. July 1964"

The End

199

Thank You!

Thanks for reading my book.

If you loved this book and have a moment to spare, I would really appreciate a short review on Amazon.com/ Kindle or my Facebook page: www.facebook.com/chrisdaleauthor.

Your help in spreading the word is gratefully received.

You can also stay up to date with my other books or new books I am writing by subscribing to my mailing list on: www.chrisdale.info/contact/ or e-mail me at: chris@chrisdale.info.

ABOUT THE AUTHOR

Chris Dale was indeed born in Lima, Peru on 7th January 1954 and most of this story is based on his early life in Lima, his experiences at a boarding school in the UK, and some – not all of the adventures are fact based. However, some poetic license has been added to make the story more of a fictional tale than a true autobiography.

Chris is now 62, and spent all of his working life in commercial sales and marketing roles in the food retailing industry, latterly running his own consultancy business, and owning and running a flying school. In July 2014, he suffered a serious stroke, which forced semi-retirement, and thus he found the joy of writing, with this being his fourth book.

The Boy from Peru

'This story is partly based on fact, from a personal experience, and partly embellished fiction; however, the names of all the people depicted in this story have been changed.

Any resemblance to names, people, characters, locations, organisations, businesses, places, events or incidents are totally and purely co-incidental and a product of the authors imagination. Any resemblance to any persons, living or dead, events or locations are entirely coincidental'

Written by Chris Dale

chris@mydale.co.uk

July 2016

Also by Chris Dale

My Stroke '… just get on with it'

Crimson Love

The 42 Million

The Bentley Regatta

The Chameleon Pilot

The Magic Christmas Table

The 14:52

Printed in Poland
by Amazon Fulfillment
Poland Sp. z o.o., Wrocław